PRAYER POWERPOINTS

To
Armin Gesswein,
beloved prayer warrior
and mentor

P R A Y E R
POWERPOINTS

COMPILED BY

RANDALL D. ROTH

VICTOR BOOKS

A DIVISION OF SCRIPTURE PRESS PUBLICATIONS INC.
USA CANADA ENGLAND

Copyediting: Barbara Williams
Cover Design: Grace K. Chan Mallette
Cover Photo: FPG International, Corp.

Library of Congress Cataloging-in-Publication Data

Prayer powerpoints / compiled by Randall D. Roth.
    p. cm.
Includes bibliographical references and index.
ISBN 1-56476-433-8
    1. Prayer—Christianity—Quotations, maxims, etc. I. Roth,
Randall D.
BV205.P73   1995
248.3'2—dc20   95-1640
                                    CIP

CONTENTS

✦ ✦ ✦

FOREWORD

✦ ✦ ✦

God's timing is always remarkable! Randy Roth's *Prayer Powerpoints* could not have come at a more strategic moment.

You see, the church of Jesus Christ worldwide finds itself, at this very moment, caught up in a movement of prayer unprecedented in history. And there's much more to come. For example, I've just returned from a gathering of 600 national leaders who came together, with only five-weeks notice, to spend three days in prayer and fasting. Day and night we prayed for God to bring a massive revival to our land. And we departed to our places of influence and service determined to labor as never before to see all of God's people actively engaged in prayer — both personal and corporate. Such a gathering has rarely, if ever, taken place in American spiritual epochs. (And this is only one of hundreds of such amazing stories unfolding right now.) As I said: God's timing is always remarkable.

Some have called this movement a "prayer awakening" — the precursor to a more generalized spiritual awakening to Christ in our generation, in answer to myriads of faithful prayers by millions of concerned Christians.

But there's a new dimension to all of this right now. We might also call this movement a "hope awakening." The church is rousing from slumber with a greater sense of impending revival — personal, national, and global. As the National Consultation on United Prayer put it: "The only hope for the nations is revival in the church. And the only hope for revival is a God-given movement of united prayer."

That being so, Christ's followers are asking for help in *two* key areas: help with wisdom and perspective on the whole (often neglected) phenomenon of prayer; *and* help in clarifying what we're to be praying about, as well as the vision we're to be praying toward.

Enter Randy Roth. In *Prayer Powerpoints* he brings us help on both concerns, and he does it in a volume that is the first of its kind. Drawing on the experience and writings of a long line of prophets of prayer, he offers us one choice nugget after another that enriches our understanding of both the *activity* of prayer and the *substance* of prayer. It's like a *university* of prayer under one cover! And what a sterling faculty Roth has assembled.

But Randy Roth is no armchair dean of prayer. He has been in the trenches of the prayer movement for a long time. Both as a pastor and as a pastor to pastors, in two major cities of our nation, Roth has promoted the call to personal and corporate (and even city-wide) prayer for nearly two decades.

Let me be personal for a moment. Back in 1982, when I was helping to launch a prayer movement in Madison, Wisconsin (where I lived at the time) Randy made contact with me from Portland, Oregon. Instantly we knew we were pursuing a similar vision. From that first phone call, we began to lead our individual prayer movements to "adopt" each other as sister cities, and to pray with equal fervor for our sister city (as a part of the prayer agenda in our individual prayer movements). From that point onward, I have had the privilege of tracking with Randy, and watching the marvelous ways God has been using him locally and nationally to foster prayer in our land, and beyond. Churches, pastors, cities, and even whole denominations now look to him for the kind of encouragement he brings to us in *Prayer Powerpoints*.

And so I urge you to take up this "university of prayer" and drink deeply of the wisdom it offers. Here you have the heartbeat of generations on the magnificent adventure of prayer. Here God can open up to you whole new vistas on your personal prayer life. Here you can find the fuel for bold, confident, victorious praying.

Here you can discover so much of what God is longing to unleash in Christ's church. Here you can step into a deepening and accelerating prayer movement that will ultimately result in nothing less than (in the words of one of our greatest preachers on prayer) "explicit agreement and visible union of all God's people in extraordinary prayer for the revival of the church and the advancement of Christ's kingdom on the earth."

Jonathan Edwards wrote that in 1748. God wants to write that today right where you live! All Randy Roth wants to do is help you get started. We need to let him.

DAVID BRYANT
Founder and President
Concerts of Prayer International

INTRODUCTION

✦ ✦ ✦

While I am not an expert on prayer, I am an answer to prayer. Only later in my life did I learn that I was the object of the prayers of godly grandparents. My Grandpa Charlie told me that Grandma Ollie, both now with the Lord, would rise daily at 5:30 A.M., roll out of bed and onto her knees. She would open her dog-eared diary and work through her prayer list, always recording and dating the answers. Grandpa told me that I was on that prayer list. She and other faithful family members kept me in their prayers throughout my rebellious early teen years, until the Hound of Heaven tracked me down and I surrendered my life to Jesus Christ as a freshman in high school. I am convinced that I would not be where I am today, were it not for prayer. The question I ask myself is, who will be the beneficiary of my prayers?

Prayer is potent. It is also difficult. Holding conversation with Someone who is invisible isn't easy. As Bill

Hybels put it, "Prayer is unnatural activity."[1] It's unnatural because prayer is by faith, not by sight. Only by faith can we move into the unseen realm of communication with God.

We struggle with prayer not only because it is unnatural, but also because it is adversarial. Prayer is warfare, and just getting to prayer is half the battle. Our flesh says, "Later." And the devil says, "Why pray when you can plan . . . organize . . . work . . . hurry . . . worry. . . ." Samuel Chadwick wrote, "The one concern of the devil is to keep Christians from praying. He fears nothing from prayerless studies, prayerless work and prayerless religion. He laughs at our toil, mocks at our wisdom, but trembles when we pray."

Getting to prayer is half the battle. Staying there is the other half. Either we fall asleep, or our mind wanders, or we get disenchanted. We don't see ready answers to our petitions, so we give up. But like any other wise investment, prayer requires the discipline of delayed gratification. The fact that Jesus knew all about the temptation to quit is evident by how He urged His disciples to "always pray and not give up. . . . Will not God bring about justice for His chosen ones, who cry out to Him day and night?" (Luke 18:1, 7)

Because I know both the potency and the problem of prayer, I need all the encouragement I can get. That's why I save and savor pithy, powerful proverbs on prayer. Call me a prayer packrat! When I discover insights on prayer I write them down in my journal. For the past ten years I have been collecting quotations on prayer for my own inspiration. I call them "Prayer Powerpoints." Now there are over 500, broken down into thirty-four subheadings. I thought I should pass on the blessing to others.

These "Prayer Powerpoints" cover the waterfront in terms of subjects and sources: from contemplative to combative; solitary to united; from great late saints like Martin Luther, to contemporary mentors in the spiritual disciplines like Richard Foster, to revival prayer mobilizers like David Bryant.

My hope is that these quintessential truths on prayer will fortify you with plenty of good reason to pray, with all kinds of prayer, and in every season.

PRAYER'S PRIORITY

✦ ✦ ✦

"I urge, then, first of all, that re-
quests, prayers, intercession and
thanksgiving be made for every-
one — for kings and all those in au-
thority, that we may live peaceful
and quiet lives in all godliness and
holiness."

1 Timothy 2:1-2

"Avail yourself of the greatest privilege
this side of heaven. Jesus Christ died to make
this communion and communication
with the Father possible."

BILLY GRAHAM

✦ ✦ ✦

"We should pray when we are in a praying
mood, for it would be sinful to neglect so fair an
opportunity. We should pray when we are not in
a proper mood, for it would be dangerous to
remain in so unhealthy a condition."

CHARLES H. SPURGEON

✦ ✦ ✦

"It is impossible for a believer, no matter
what his experience, to keep right with God
if he will not take the trouble to spend time
with God. Spend plenty of time with Him;
let other things go, but don't neglect Him."

OSWALD CHAMBERS

✦ ✦ ✦

"The testimony of the great souls is a
clear affirmation of this: some things
never without thinking; some things
never without working; some things never
without praying! Prayer is one of the three
forms of man's cooperation with God."

HARRY EMERSON FOSDICK

"Prayer is the nearest approach to God
and the highest enjoyment of Him that
we are capable of in this life."[1]

WILLIAM LAW

✦ ✦ ✦

"Neglect prayer. Neglect God."[2]

O. HALLESBY

✦ ✦ ✦

"None but praying leaders can have
praying followers . . . we do greatly
need somebody who can set the saints
to this business of praying."

E.M. BOUNDS

✦ ✦ ✦

"Give me one hundred preachers who
fear nothing but sin, and desire nothing
but God, and I care not a straw whether
they be clergymen or laymen; such alone
will shake the gates of Hell and set up
the Kingdom of Heaven on earth."[3]

JOHN WESLEY

✦ ✦ ✦

"Prayer is not everything,
but everything is by prayer."[4]

RAY ORTLUND

"God will do nothing on earth except
in answer to believing prayer."

JOHN WESLEY

✦ ✦ ✦

"Prayer is to religion what original
research is to science."

P.T. FORSYTH

✦ ✦ ✦

"To pray is to change. Prayer is the central
avenue God uses to transform us . . . real
prayer is life creating and life changing."[5]

RICHARD FOSTER

✦ ✦ ✦

"Nothing I can do will please Christ more than
my joining with Him in daily prayer. And when I
do, something happens in the world that could
not happen through any other means."[6]

DICK EASTMAN

✦ ✦ ✦

"The men who have done the most for God in
this world have been those who have been early
on their knees. He who fritters away the early
morning, its opportunity and freshness, in other
pursuits than seeking God will make poor
headway seeking Him the rest of the day."

E.M. BOUNDS

"Prayer is the putting forth of vital energy.
It is the highest effort of which
the human spirit is capable."

ANDREW MURRAY

✦ ✦ ✦

"We have forgotten that when Christ built His
church, He built a prayer meeting!"[7]

ARMIN GESSWEIN

✦ ✦ ✦

"Five minutes with Him in which the soul is
touched by the forces of eternity will mean
a day full of spiritual vigor. God can do
much in five minutes of a man's time if no
more can honestly be spared. He can do
nothing in five minutes for the man who
should give Him sixty, but who is slothful."

G. CAMPBELL MORGAN

✦ ✦ ✦

"It is not wasted time to wait upon God."

J. HUDSON TAYLOR

✦ ✦ ✦

"To be a Christian without prayer is no more
possible than to be alive without breathing."

MARTIN LUTHER

"Mastering the art of prayer, like any other art,
will take time, and the amount of time we
allocate to it will be the true measure of
our conception of its importance."

J. OSWALD SANDERS

✦ ✦ ✦

"Prayer is the contemplation of life
from the highest point of view."

WILLIAM JAMES

✦ ✦ ✦

"The men upon whose shoulders rested the
initial responsibility of Christianizing
the world came to Jesus with one supreme
request. They did not say, 'Lord, teach us
to preach'; 'Lord, teach us to do miracles,'
or 'Lord, teach us to be wise' . . . but
they said, 'Lord, teach us to pray.' "[8]

BILLY GRAHAM

✦ ✦ ✦

"A watch was running slow. The watchmaker
asked when the owner wound it,
and when told 'at night,' replied,
'Wind it in the morning. Give it the fresh spring
at the hardest part of the day,
when you are moving about.' Give your soul
the fresh spring of the Morning Watch

before you go out and face the hard part of the
day the daily tasks and problems."[9]

E. STANLEY JONES

✦ ✦ ✦

"What wings are to a bird, and sails to
a ship, is prayer to the soul."[10]

CORRIE TEN BOOM

✦ ✦ ✦

"As a camel kneels before his master
to have him remove his burden at the
end of the day, so kneel each night
and let the Master take your burden."[11]

CORRIE TEN BOOM

✦ ✦ ✦

"Prayer is and remains the native and
deepest impulse of the soul of man."

THOMAS CARLYLE

✦ ✦ ✦

"If I should neglect prayer but a single day, I
should lose a great deal of the fire of faith."

MARTIN LUTHER

✦ ✦ ✦

"Perfume all your actions with the
life-giving breath of prayer."

POPE JOHN XXIII

"Whether we like it or not, asking is
the rule of the kingdom."

CHARLES H. SPURGEON

✦ ✦ ✦

"Prayer is where the action is.
Any church without a well organized
and systematic prayer program
is simply operating a religious treadmill."[12]

PAUL BILLHEIMER

✦ ✦ ✦

"God seeks intercessors. God needs
intercessors. God wonders why there are
not more intercessors. Do not rest
until God sees that *you* are one."[13]

ANDREW MURRAY

✦ ✦ ✦

"I have been driven many times to my knees by
the overwhelming conviction that I had nowhere else to go. My own wisdom, and that of
all about me, seemed insufficient for that day."

ABRAHAM LINCOLN

✦ ✦ ✦

"If we think of prayer as the breath in our lungs
and the blood from our hearts, we think rightly.

The blood flows ceaselessly, and breathing
continues ceaselessly; we are not
conscious of it, but it is always going on."[14]

OSWALD CHAMBERS

✦ ✦ ✦

"The moment you wake up each morning,
all your wishes and hopes for the day
rush at you like wild animals.
And the first job each morning consists
in shoving it all back; in listening
to that other voice, taking that other
point of view, letting that other, larger,
stronger, quieter life come flowing in."

C.S. LEWIS

✦ ✦ ✦

"Prayer is the key of the morning
and the bolt of the evening."

MATTHEW HENRY

✦ ✦ ✦

"Pray for great things, expect great things,
work for great things, but above all, pray."

R.A. TORREY

✦ ✦ ✦

"I have so much to do today that I shall
spend the first three hours in prayer."

MARTIN LUTHER

"He who rushes from his bed
to his business and waiteth not
to worship in prayer, is as foolish
as though he had not put on
his clothes or washed his face and as unwise
as though he dashed into battle
without arms or armor."

ANONYMOUS

✦ ✦ ✦

"God will not do apart from prayer
what He says He will only do
in answer to prayer."

ARMIN GESSWEIN

✦ ✦ ✦

"Just as the business of the tailor is
to make clothes, and that of the shoemaker
to mend shoes, so the business of
the Christian is to pray."

MARTIN LUTHER

✦ ✦ ✦

"What the church needs today is not
more machinery or better, not new organiza-
tions or more and novel methods, but men
whom the Holy Spirit can use —
men of prayer, men mighty in prayer."

E.M. BOUNDS

"I am convinced that nothing can avail,
except churches and ministers on their knees
in total dependence on God.
As long as you go on organizing,
people will not fall on their knees
and implore God to come
and heal them."

MARTYN LLOYD-JONES

✦ ✦ ✦

"Prayer is an all-efficient panoply,
a treasure undiminished, a mine
which is never exhausted,
a sky unobscured by clouds,
a heaven unruffled by the storm.
It is the root, the fountain,
the mother of a thousand blessings."

CHRYSOSTOM

✦ ✦ ✦

"God shapes the world by prayer."[15]

E.M. BOUNDS

✦ ✦ ✦

"It is staggering to even begin to realize
that the whole process by which God's will
is done on earth depends on
an interceding church."[16]

JACK HAYFORD

"Until we believe that prayer is indeed
a real and highly significant activity,
that it does in fact reach beyond space and time
to the God who is actually there, we will never
acquire the habits of worship and intercession.
In order to gain these habits,
we must make a conscious effort to
overcome the part of us that thinks that
praying is not a natural part of life."[17]

GORDON MACDONALD

✦ ✦ ✦

"It's so easy to promise to pray for people, or
just plan to pray for people, and forget. So
many afflictions, so many tragedies or desperate hopes that cry out for intercession. Only an
instant of my time, only a few words, a
thought — and who knows? It may be the only
word of prayer that person will get."[18]

MARJORIE HOLMES

✦ ✦ ✦

"God expects us to be orderly. He expects us to
manage our time, to discipline ourselves, to
prepare well-planned programs, but if we could
learn to pray first and plan afterward, how different would be our homes, our churches, our
Christian women's clubs, our Bible studies,
whatever we are doing for Christ."[19]

EVELYN CHRISTENSON

"You can do more than pray,
after you have prayed, but you can never do
more than pray until you have prayed."

A.J. GORDON

✦ ✦ ✦

"Believe me, prayer is our highest privilege,
our gravest responsibility, and greatest
power God has put into our hands.
Prayer, real prayer, is the noblest,
the sublimest, the most stupendous act
that any creature of God can perform."[20]

THE KNEELING CHRISTIAN

✦ ✦ ✦

"In one year, Christianity lost three holy women
of faith, Agnes Sanford, Corrie ten Boom and
Catherine Marshall — as well as countless others
whose names are unknown but who nevertheless
did the work of God in this world. These are
the women who knew what it meant to experience
the presence of the unseen, who spent hours
on their knees, who wept over the wounds
of the world. For them, prayer was a second language. Who will take their place?"[21]

KAREN BURTON MAINS

✦ ✦ ✦

"It is a great art to commune with God."

THOMAS à KEMPIS

"A man without prayer is like a
tree without roots."

POPE PIUS XII

✦ ✦ ✦

"All the Christian virtues are locked up
in the word prayer."

CHARLES SPURGEON

✦ ✦ ✦

"Prayer is not something we do at a specific time,
but something we do all the time."

RICHARD OWEN ROBERTS

PRAYER'S PURPOSE

✦ ✦ ✦

"One thing I ask of the Lord, this
is what I seek: that I may dwell in
the house of the Lord all the days
of my life, to gaze upon the beauty
of the Lord and to seek Him in His
temple."

Psalm 27:4

"It's not only to resolve
our problems that we should pray,
but to share in the strength
of God's friendship.
For us, prayer should be not
merely an act, but
an attitude of life."

BILLY GRAHAM

✦ ✦ ✦

"Prayer is an unnatural activity."[1]

BILL HYBELS

✦ ✦ ✦

"The purpose of prayer is not
to get man's will done in heaven,
but to get God's will
done on earth."

WARREN WIERSBE

✦ ✦ ✦

"Prayer is not conquering God's reluctance,
but taking hold of God's willingness."

PHILLIPS BROOKS

✦ ✦ ✦

"Prayer is conversation with God."

CLEMENT OF ALEXANDRIA

"A good deal of our praying probably
accomplishes little because it is not specific.
Pointless prayer is faithless prayer."

DICK EASTMAN

✦ ✦ ✦

"The mind is constituted that it cannot fasten
its desires intensely upon many things at the
same time. All the instances of effective prayer
recorded in the Bible are of this kind. Wherever
you see that the blessing sought for in prayer
was attained, you will find that the prayer which
was offered was prayer for that definite object."

CHARLES FINNEY

✦ ✦ ✦

"When you pray, rather let your heart be without
words than your words without heart."

JOHN BUNYAN

✦ ✦ ✦

"The purpose of all prayer is to find God's will
and to make that will our prayer."

CATHERINE MARSHALL

✦ ✦ ✦

"He could have bestowed these things on us
even without our prayers;

but He wished that by our prayers we should
be taught from where these benefits come."

AUGUSTINE

✦ ✦ ✦

"Prayer enlarges the heart until it is
capable of containing God's gift of Himself."[2]

MOTHER TERESA

✦ ✦ ✦

"The heart of prayer is not to alter God's will
but to find it."

SAM SHOEMAKER

✦ ✦ ✦

"The fundamental law in prayer is this:
Prayer is given and ordained for the
purpose of glorifying God."

O. HALLESBY

✦ ✦ ✦

"When a man is born from above,
the life of the Son of God is born in him,
and he can either starve that life or nourish it.
Prayer is the way the life of God
is nourished."

OSWALD CHAMBERS

"The possibilities of prayer are found in its ally-
ing itself with the purposes of God, for God's
purposes and man's praying are the combination of all potent and omnipotent forces."[3]

E.M. BOUNDS

✦ ✦ ✦

"Prayer is the moment when heaven and earth
kiss each other."

OLD JEWISH PROVERB

✦ ✦ ✦

"Intercession is simply love at prayer."

THE KNEELING CHRISTIAN

✦ ✦ ✦

"Prayer is an offering up of our desires unto
God, for things agreeable to His will, in the
name of Christ, with confession of our sins, and
thankful acknowledgment of His mercies."[4]

WESTMINSTER SHORTER CATECHISM

✦ ✦ ✦

"It is not that prayer changes God, or awakens
in Him purposes of love and compassion that
He has not already felt. No, it changes us, and
therein lies its glory and its purpose."

HANNAH HURNARD

"Prayer is not an argument with God to persuade Him to move things our way, but an exercise by which we are enabled by His Spirit to move ourselves His way."

LEONARD RAVENHILL

PRAYER POWER

✦ ✦ ✦

"After they prayed, the place where they were meeting was shaken. And they were all filled with the Holy Spirit and spoke the word of God boldly."

Acts 4:31

"When I get on my knees, God helps me
to stand up to anything."

ANONYMOUS

✦ ✦ ✦

"I can take my telescope and look millions of
miles into space, but I can lay it aside
and go into my room, shut the door,
get down on my knees in earnest prayer,
and see more of heaven and get closer to God
than I can assisted by all the telescopes
and material agencies on earth."

SIR ISAAC NEWTON

✦ ✦ ✦

"Prayer is a powerful thing, for God
has bound and tied Himself thereto."

MARTIN LUTHER

✦ ✦ ✦

"Prayer will change circumstances or
prayer will change you."

ANONYMOUS

✦ ✦ ✦

"Prayers have no boundaries. They can leap
miles and continents and be translated
instantly into any language."[1]

BILLY GRAHAM

"Certain things will happen in history if we pray rightly. We are to change the world by prayer. What more motivation do we need to learn this loftiest human exercise?"

RICHARD FOSTER

✦ ✦ ✦

"When I pray, coincidences happen."

WILLIAM TEMPLE

✦ ✦ ✦

"Prayer is power when pardoned people pray."[2]

MELVA WICKMAN

✦ ✦ ✦

"A day hemmed in prayer seldom unravels."

ANONYMOUS

✦ ✦ ✦

"Intercession is the link between man's impotence and God's omnipotence."

ANDREW MURRAY

✦ ✦ ✦

"More things are wrought by prayer than this world dreams of."

SIR ALFRED LORD TENNYSON

"Jesus didn't pray about things,
He brought things about by prayer."[3]

ARMIN GESSWEIN

✦ ✦ ✦

"John Knox was a man famous for his power in
prayer, so that Queen Mary of England
used to say that she feared his prayer
more than all the armies of Europe."

CHARLES FINNEY

✦ ✦ ✦

"There is no power like that of prevailing prayer.
It turns ordinary mortals into men of power."

SAMUEL CHADWICK

✦ ✦ ✦

"Prayer can change anything. The impossible
doesn't exist. His is the power.
Ours is the prayer. Without Him, we cannot.
Without us, He will not."[4]

JACK HAYFORD

✦ ✦ ✦

"None can believe how powerful prayer is,
and what it is able to effect,
but those who have learned it by experience."

MARTIN LUTHER

"Prayer is that slender nerve
that moves the muscles of omnipotence."[5]

CHARLES SPURGEON

✦ ✦ ✦

"At the death of Robert McCheyne, the Scottish
preacher, someone said, 'Perhaps the heaviest
blow to his brethren, his people and the land,
is the loss of his intercession.'"

HARRY EMERSON FOSDICK

✦ ✦ ✦

"Units of prayer combined, like drops of water,
make an ocean which defies resistance."[6]

E.M. BOUNDS

✦ ✦ ✦

"The globe itself lives and is upheld as by Atlas'
arms through the prayers of those whose love
has not grown cold. The world lives by these up-
lifted hands, and by nothing else."

HELMUT THIELICKE

✦ ✦ ✦

"Prayer is able to prevail with Heaven and
bend omnipotence to its desires."

CHARLES SPURGEON

"God has instituted prayer so as
to confer upon His creatures the dignity
of being causes."

BLAISE PASCAL

✦ ✦ ✦

"Prayer is the conduit through which power
from heaven is brought to earth."[7]

O. HALLESBY

✦ ✦ ✦

"You can love more people through prayer
than any other way. You can love,
by your prayer, people who avoid you
or resist you. You can love people anywhere
in the world by your prayer. The more
you pour out God's love through your prayer
and actions, the more the Spirit
will pour in as you ask Him."[8]

WESLEY DUEWEL

✦ ✦ ✦

"From one end of the Bible to the other,
we find the record of people
whose prayers have been answered —
people who turned the tide of history
by prayer, men who prayed fervently and
whom God answered."[9]

BILLY GRAHAM

"Prayer is a different avenue to power. Our age
is power-conscious, but many have yet to
discover that this is the most powerful power
of all. We can pray from any depth of need,
from any hellhole of sin, from any distance
of skepticism and unbelief whatsoever.
A cry to God in the darkness
is heard by Him in the light."[10]

SAM SHOEMAKER

✦ ✦ ✦

"Prayer is the easiest and the hardest of all
things; the simplest and the sublimest; the
weakest and the most powerful; its results lie
outside the range of human possibilities; they
are limited only by the omnipotence of God."[11]

E.M. BOUNDS

✦ ✦ ✦

"The whole field of prayer, and praying as laying
hold on unlimited power, is unexplored, with
the result that spiritual laws still lie
undiscovered by the average believer."

PETER MARSHALL

✦ ✦ ✦

"Luther and his companions were men
of such mighty pleading with God, that they
broke the spell of ages, and laid nations subdued

at the foot of the Cross. John Knox grasped
all Scotland in his strong arms of faith
and his prayers terrified tyrants. Whitefield,
after much bold, faithful closet pleading,
went to the devil's playground and
took more than a thousand souls
out of the paws of the lion
in one day."

D.L. MOODY

✦ ✦ ✦

"We're under instructions to change the world.
Once you have been rescued from it,
you'll need power to become a threat
to it. The world which contained you
in its grasp until now will not release
its hold on others without a fight.
Power is the key to victory,
and prayer is the pathway to power."[12]

JACK HAYFORD

✦ ✦ ✦

"The key for the empowerment
of the church . . . is
the moving of the Holy Spirit in the midst
of a worshiping, prayerful community
of God's people. Only then can the church
be the church."[13]

CHARLES COLSON

"If all regenerate church members in Western Christendom were to intercede daily simply for the most obvious spiritual concerns visible in their homes, their workplaces, their local churches and denominations, their nations, and the world . . . the transformation which would result would be incalculable."[14]

RICHARD LOVELACE

✦ ✦ ✦

"When people start praying together in one accord to our Father in heaven, in the name of Jesus, and practice praying together, things begin to change. Our lives change, our families change, our churches change, our communities change. Changes take place not when we study about prayer, not when we talk about it, not even when we memorize beautiful Scripture verses on prayer; it is when we actually pray that things begin to happen."[15]

EVELYN CHRISTENSON

✦ ✦ ✦

"My life is one long, daily, hourly record of answered prayer for physical health, for mental overstrain, for guidance given marvelously, for errors and dangers averted, for enmity to the Gospel subdued, for food provided at the exact hour needed,

for everything that goes to make up life
and my poor service. I can testify with
a full and often wonder-stricken awe
that I believe God answers prayer.
I know God answers prayer!"

MARY SLESSOR

+ + +

"Prayer is such an important power.
In the concentration camp, seven hundred of us
lived in a room built for two hundred people.
We were all dirty, nervous and tense. One day
a horrible fight broke out amongst
the prisoners. Betsie began to pray aloud.
It was as if a storm laid down, until at last
all was quiet. Then Betsie said, 'Thank you,
Father.' A tired old woman was used by
the Lord to save the situation for
seven hundred fellow prisoners through
her prayers."[16]

CORRIE TEN BOOM

+ + +

"He is not deaf, He listens: more than that, He
acts. He does not act in the same way whether
we pray or not. Prayer exerts an influence
upon God's action, even upon His existence.
This is what the word 'answer' means."[17]

KARL BARTH

✦ ✦

"To this day the prayer level is the power
level of the church. Our prayer meetings
give us away. When the knees are not
often bent the feet soon slide!"[18]

ARMIN GESSWEIN

✦ ✦ ✦

"The Lord is great and high, and therefore
He wants great things to be sought from Him
and is willing to bestow them so that His
almighty power might be shown forth."[19]

MARTIN LUTHER

✦ ✦ ✦

"Our prayers lay the track down which
God's power can come. Like a mighty
locomotive His power is irresistible,
but it cannot reach us without rails."

WATCHMAN NEE

✦ ✦ ✦

"Prayer can do anything God can do."

E.M. BOUNDS

✦ ✦ ✦

"The spectacle of a nation praying is more awe-
inspiring than the explosion of an atomic
bomb. The force of prayer is greater than any

possible combination of man-controlled powers because prayer is man's greatest means of tapping the infinite resources of God."[20]

J. EDGAR HOOVER

✦ ✦ ✦

"Thou art coming to a King
Large petitions with thee bring;
For His grace and power are such
None can ever ask too much."

JOHN NEWTON

✦ ✦ ✦

"When in prayer you clasp your hands,
God opens His."

GERMAN PROVERB

✦ ✦ ✦

"When you pray you get in on God's will before it happens."[21]

DELORES JARVIS

4

PRAYER PRIORITIES

✦ ✦ ✦

"This is how you should pray:

'Our Father in heaven,
hallowed be Your name,
Your kingdom come,
Your will be done
on earth as it is in heaven.
Give us today our daily bread.
Forgive us our debts,
as we also have forgiven
    our debtors.
And lead us not into temptation,
but deliver us from the evil one.' "

Matthew 6:9-13

"He prays not at all in whose prayer
there is no mention of the
Kingdom of God."

OLD JEWISH PROVERB

✦ ✦ ✦

"Quality prayer is prayer
that seeks God first
and 'answers' second."

DICK EASTMAN

✦ ✦ ✦

"Before you pray for a change
of circumstances, you should pray
for a change in character."[1]

JOHN ALLAN LAVENDER

✦ ✦ ✦

"It is necessary that in our general prayers
for others we should not exclude our enemies."[2]

THOMAS AQUINAS

✦ ✦ ✦

"We say we believe God to be omniscient;
but a great deal of prayer seems to consist
of giving Him information."[3]

C.S. LEWIS

"Do not pray for tasks
equal to your powers. Pray for powers
equal to your tasks."

PHILLIPS BROOKS

+ + +

"Prayer is to intercede for the well-being
of others before God."

AUGUSTINE

+ + +

"Intercession leaves you neither time
nor inclination to pray for your own
'sad sweet self.' The thought of yourself
is not kept out, because it is not there
to keep out; you are completely and
entirely identified with God's interests
in other lives."[4]

OSWALD CHAMBERS

+ + +

"It's not wrong to pray for miracles.
But it is wrong to insist upon our own will
rather than God's. We may not demand miracles
of a sovereign God. Unfortunately,
such demands are made in all too many
Christian circles today."

MARGARET CLARKSON

"Many of us have discovered that true prayer begins where we can begin to say with Jesus, 'Not my will, but Thine be done.' That should not mean mere resignation to fate, it should mean cooperation with the will of God."[5]

SAM SHOEMAKER

✦ ✦ ✦

"We as a church pray not because it is the key to something—healing the sick, church growth, or even revival—but because God is God and worthy of our total obedience and reverence."[6]

CHARLES COLSON

✦ ✦ ✦

"Pray so that there is a real continuity between your prayer and your whole actual life."[7]

P.T. FORSYTH

✦ ✦ ✦

"Prayer should rise more out of God's Word and concern for His kingdom than even out of our personal needs, trials or desires."[8]

P.T. FORSYTH

✦ ✦ ✦

"If we will make use of prayer, not to wrest from God advantages for ourselves or our dear ones,

or to escape from tribulations and difficulties,
but to call down upon ourselves and others
those things which will glorify the name of God,
then we should see the strongest and boldest
promises of the Bible about prayer fulfilled also
in our weak, little prayer life."[9]

O. HALLESBY

✦ ✦ ✦

"Pray for the highest of all gifts, for the gift of divine love. It is a never-ending love, for it is the
chief attribute of God and therefore imperish-
able like God himself. This love is to be yours."[10]

BASILEA SCHLINK

PRAYER AND WORK

✦ ✦ ✦

"In the same way, faith by itself, if it is not accompanied by action, is dead."

James 2:17

"It is not prayer in addition to work, but prayer
simultaneous with work. We precede, enfold
and follow all our work with prayer."[1]

RICHARD FOSTER

✦ ✦ ✦

"All Christians are obligated to work as if
they do not believe in prayer and pray
as if they do not believe in work."

LEONARD RAVENHILL

✦ ✦ ✦

"Not to work and then to pray to make up for it
I consider to be bad manners."

CHARLES PEGUY

✦ ✦ ✦

"Prayer without work is like an empty wagon —
lots of noise but no load."

ANONYMOUS

✦ ✦ ✦

"How misguided are those who regard prayer as
irrelevant to social conditions! . . . nothing
is more relevant to social conditions
than the transformation of persons that
comes from prayer at its best in
the life of the disciples of Christ."[2]

DALLAS WILLARD

"The sin of doing and not praying is only rivaled
by the sin of praying and not doing."

ANONYMOUS

✦ ✦ ✦

"Prayer must take the place of anxiety
and must underlie our work for the morrow.
The children of God are not anxious about work;
they work because they pray."[3]

KARL BARTH

✦ ✦ ✦

"Work as if you were to live a hundred years.
Pray as if you were to die tomorrow."

BENJAMIN FRANKLIN

✦ ✦ ✦

"Intercession is truly universal work for the
Christian. No place is closed to intercessory
prayer. No continent — no nation — no organization — no city — no office. There is no power on
earth that can keep intercession out."[4]

RICHARD C. HALVERSON

✦ ✦ ✦

"There is a way of ordering our mental life
on more than one level at once. On one level
we may be thinking, discussing, seeing,

calculating, meeting all the demands of
external affairs. But deep within,
behind the scenes, at a profounder level,
we may also be in prayer and adoration,
song and worship and a gentle reception
to divine breathings."[5]

THOMAS KELLY

✦ ✦ ✦

"Prayer is like any other work; we may not feel
like working, but once we have been at it for a
bit, we begin to feel like working."[6]

RICHARD FOSTER

✦ ✦ ✦

"Every work of God can be traced to
some kneeling form."

D.L. MOODY

✦ ✦ ✦

"Not just pray about the work.
Prayer is the work."[7]

ARMIN GESSWEIN

✦ ✦ ✦

"When we work, we work.
When we pray, God works."

J. HUDSON TAYLOR

"As far as my understanding of these things
goes, intercessory prayer is the finest
and most exacting kind of work
that is possible for men to perform."

O. HALLESBY

✦ ✦ ✦

"Prayer does not just fit us for the greater work.
Prayer is the greater work."

J. OSWALD CHAMBERS

✦ ✦ ✦

"Prayer is the gymnasium of the soul."

SAMUEL ZWEMER

✦ ✦ ✦

"Prayer should never be an excuse
for inaction. Nehemiah prayed, but
he also set watches for protection —
he used common sense. As a result,
what had not been done in a hundred years'
time was finished in fifty-two days."[8]

CORRIE TEN BOOM

✦ ✦ ✦

"As a rain-cloud brings the shower, so prayer
brings the blessing. As spring scatters flowers,
so supplication ensures mercies.

In all labor there is profit, but most of all
in the work of intercession I am sure of this,
for I have reaped it."[9]

C.H. SPURGEON

✦ ✦ ✦

"The time of business does not
with me differ from the time of prayer,
and in the noise and clutter of my kitchen,
while several persons are at the same time
calling for different things, I possess God
in as great tranquility as if I were upon my knees
at the blessed sacrament."[10]

BROTHER LAWRENCE

✦ ✦ ✦

"Clearly we must not pray for any end
towards which it is wrong to labour,
but likewise we must not labour
towards any end for which
it is wrong to pray."

JOHN BAILLIE

✦ ✦ ✦

"You can do more than pray after you've prayed,
but you cannot do more than pray
until you have prayed."

JOHN BUNYAN

"We need to realize that prayer is not just
for personal use, nor is it only for
devotional purpose. Prayer is a ministry.
Prayer is work."[11]

WATCHMAN NEE

✦ ✦ ✦

"The prayer of the Christian reaches
beyond its set time and extends into the heart
of his work. It includes the whole day,
and in doing so, it does not hinder the work;
it promotes it, affirms it, and lends it
meaning and joy."[12]

DIETRICH BONHOEFFER

✦ ✦ ✦

"Get out your atlas and your National
Geographic and a good newspaper and
start praying for the basic needs of people
so much more desperate than most of us.
Let your heart be broken for a world in need.
Stretch yourself to reach out beyond
your own requirements. And make sure
that you are ready to help meet needs
when God wants to use you. For prayer is
never meant to be a substitute for action, and
action always needs the stabilizing influence
of prayer."[13]

BRYAN JEFFERY LEECH

"As we pray for increase of strength or virtue,
let us remember that the answer is likely to
take the form of opportunity to exercise it, like
the lady who prayed for patience and was
provided with an ill-tempered cook."

WILLIAM TEMPLE

✦ ✦ ✦

"The best and most wonderful thing that can
happen to you in this life, is that you should
be silent and let God work . . ."[14]

DAG HAMMARSKJOLD

✦ ✦ ✦

"The right relation between prayer and conduct
is not that conduct is supremely important
and prayer may help it, but that prayer is
supremely important and conduct tests it."

WILLIAM TEMPLE

✦ ✦ ✦

"Prayer, genuine and victorious, is continually
offered without the least physical effort
or disturbance. It is often in the deepest
stillness of soul and body that it wins
its longest way. But there is another side
of the matter. Prayer is never meant to be
indolently easy, however simple and reliant
it may be. It is meant to be an infinitely

important transaction between man and God.
And therefore, very often . . . it has
to be viewed as a work involving labour,
persistence, conflict if it would be
prayer indeed."

BISHOP MOULE

✦ ✦ ✦

"What we plant in the soil of contemplation
we shall reap in the harvest of action . . ."[15]

MEISTER ECKHART

✦ ✦ ✦

"The seeming inactivity of prayer on the hill
proved to be a greater test of spiritual stamina
than fighting in the valley.
It was Moses who tired, not Joshua."[16]

J. OSWALD SANDERS

✦ ✦ ✦

"Our Lord in His teaching always made prayer,
not preparation for work, but *the* work."[17]

OSWALD CHAMBERS

✦ ✦ ✦

"To pray is to work."

BENEDICTINE MOTTO

"We see the hypocrisy of those who profess
to be praying for a revival while they are
doing nothing to promote it. There are many
who appear to be very zealous in praying
for revival while they are not doing anything
at all for one. . . . What would
you think of the farmer who should pray for
a crop, and not plow nor sow?"

CHARLES FINNEY

✦ ✦ ✦

"He who labors as he prays, lifts his heart
to God with his hands."

BERNARD OF CLAIRVAUX

✦ ✦ ✦

"I am often praying for others when I should
be doing things for them. It's so much easier to
pray for a bore than to go and see him."[18]

C.S. LEWIS

PRAYER AND FAITH

✦ ✦ ✦

"Therefore I tell you, whatever you ask for in prayer, believe that you have received it, and it will be yours."

Mark 11:24

"God doesn't demand that we pray in
King James English, or even with eloquence.
Every feeble, stumbling prayer
uttered by a believer is
heard by God."[1]

BILLY GRAHAM

✦ ✦ ✦

"Prayer is more than a wish; it is
the voice of faith directed to God."[2]

BILLY GRAHAM

✦ ✦ ✦

"Prayer is asking for rain.
Faith is carrying the umbrella."

ROBERT C. SAVAGE

✦ ✦ ✦

"Mark this! Make your amen strong,
never doubting that God is surely listening
to you. This is what amen means;
that I know with certainty that this prayer
has been heard by God."

MARTIN LUTHER

✦ ✦ ✦

"One cannot pray uncertainly."

MARTIN LUTHER

"The power of prayer rests in the faith
that God hears it. The moment I am assured
that God hears, I feel drawn to pray
and to persevere in prayer."

ANDREW MURRAY

✦ ✦ ✦

"Prayer projects faith on God, and God
on the world. Only God can move mountains,
but faith and prayer moves God."

E.M. BOUNDS

✦ ✦ ✦

"If you pray for bread and bring no basket
to carry it, you prove the doubting spirit
which may be the only hindrance to the gift
you ask."

D.L. MOODY

✦ ✦ ✦

"Helplessness united with faith
produces prayer."[3]

O. HALLESBY

✦ ✦ ✦

"Prayer is the Living Word in lips of faith."[4]

E.W. KENYON

"Prayer and faith are Siamese twins. One heart animates them both. Faith is always praying. Prayer is always believing."[5]

E.M. BOUNDS

✦ ✦ ✦

"If I should neglect prayer but a single day, I should lose a great deal of the fire of faith."

MARTIN LUTHER

✦ ✦ ✦

"Perhaps the most blessed element in this asking and getting from God lies in the strengthening of faith which comes when a definite request has been granted. What is more helpful and inspiring than a ringing testimony of *what God has done*?"

ROSALIND GOFORTH

✦ ✦ ✦

"You can take an empty cup and go to the kitchen faucet to get a drink. You can stand there all day, knowing the water is there, but you will never get one drop in your cup until you reach out and turn on the faucet. It's putting impetus to our prayer. We can pray for years and not see much happen. But when we learn to turn our prayers on by believing God, we will see what great things He can do in and through us."[6]

HOPE MACDONALD

"You must pray in faith. You must expect to obtain the things for which you ask. You need not
look for an answer to prayer, if you pray without
any expectation of obtaining it."[7]

CHARLES FINNEY

✦ ✦ ✦

"It matters little what form of prayer
we adopt or how many words we use,
what matters is the faith which lays hold
on God and touches the heart of the Father
who knew us long before we came to Him."[8]

DIETRICH BONHOEFFER

✦ ✦ ✦

"The faith we bring to prayer must include
a trust that God is able to hear our prayers
and that He is disposed to answer them.
Yet when God says no to our requests,
this faith also trusts in His wisdom."[9]

R.C. SPROUL

✦ ✦ ✦

"Faith is the omnipotent lever which exalts the
valleys and levels the mountains. . . . Faith
opens the gates for the King of glory to come in,
and when He is in, it takes hold of His strength
to pull the pillars of hell down.
Oh, let nothing frighten you, or lure you

from trust! This is the difference between
a conqueror and a coward."

CATHERINE BOOTH

✦ ✦ ✦

"In order to make sure that we are not retreating
from the tension of faith, it is helpful
to ask ourselves as we pray, 'Do I really
expect anything to happen?' This will prevent
us from going window-shopping in prayer."[10]

CATHERINE MARSHALL

✦ ✦ ✦

"Murmuring with the mouth is easy, or looks
easy. But to fill the words with sincerity of the
heart in diligent devotion, i.e., desire and faith,
so that we seriously desire what the words contain and do not doubt that the prayer is heard,
that is a great work in the sight of God."

MARTIN LUTHER

✦ ✦ ✦

"There is a vast difference between prayer in
faith and faith in prayer. Faith in prayer is very
common; almost everybody has more or less of
it. Prayer in faith is anything but common; so
uncommon, in fact, that our Lord questions if
He shall find any of it on the earth when He
comes back again."[11]

H. CLAY TRUMBELL

PRAYERLESSNESS AND BUSYNESS

✦ ✦ ✦

" 'Martha, Martha,' the Lord answered, 'you are worried and upset
about many things, but only one
thing is needed. Mary has chosen
what is better, and it will not be
taken away from her.' "

Luke 10:41-42

"Prayerlessness is expatriation, or worse,
from God's Kingdom. It is outlawry,
a high crime, a constitutional breach."[1]

E.M. BOUNDS

✦ ✦ ✦

"How many of you are praying
consistently with your children at home?
How ironic that we can seek to legislate prayer
in schools when we do not
pray at home."[2]

RICHARD C. HALVERSON

✦ ✦ ✦

"If there are any tears in Heaven, they will be
over the fact that we prayed so little."

ANONYMOUS

✦ ✦ ✦

"Heaven must be full of answers for which
no one ever bothered to ask."

CAMERON THOMPSON

✦ ✦ ✦

"The prayerless life cannot cope with
the attacks of corruption within
and the crushing blows without."

LEROY EIMS

"Prevailing apostles produce prayer warriors.
Comparatively prayerless pulpits will
produce prayerless and powerless
congregations.
Who will call today's generation
to prayer and teach them to pray?"[3]

WESLEY DUEWEL

✦ ✦ ✦

"I can be active and pray; I can work and pray;
but I cannot be busy and pray."

EUGENE PETERSON

✦ ✦ ✦

"It is nothing but the sin of prayerlessness
which is the cause of the lack of a
powerful spiritual life. . . . Oh, that all thought
and work and expectation concerning
the Kingdom might drive us to the
acknowledgment of the sin of prayerlessness!
The Lord lay the burden of it so heavy
on our hearts that we may not rest
until it is taken far from us
through the name and power of Jesus."[4]

ANDREW MURRAY

✦ ✦ ✦

"I must secure more time for private devotions.
I have been living far too public for me.

The shortening of private devotions
starves the soul, it grows lean and faint.
I have been keeping too late hours."

WILLIAM WILBERFORCE

✦ ✦ ✦

"Now the disquieting thing is not simply that
we skimp and begrudge the duty of prayer.
The really disquieting thing is it should
have to be numbered among duties at all.
For we believe that we were created
to glorify God and enjoy Him forever."[5]

C.S. LEWIS

✦ ✦ ✦

"How little time the average Christian spends in
prayer! We are too busy to pray, and so we are
too busy to have power. We have a great deal of
activity, but we accomplish little. . . . The power
of God is lacking in our lives and in our work.
We have not because we ask not."

R.A. TORREY

✦ ✦ ✦

"God's acquaintance is not made hurriedly.
He does not bestow His gifts on the
casual or hasty comer and goer. To be
much alone with God is the secret of
knowing Him and of influence with Him."

E.M. BOUNDS

"The church has many organizers but
few agonizers. Many who pay, but few who pray;
many resters but few wrestlers; many
who are enterprising, but few
who are interceding. The ministry of prayer
is open to every child of God.
In the matter of effective praying,
never have so many left so much to so few."

LEONARD RAVENHILL

✦ ✦ ✦

"Hurry is the death of prayer."

SAMUEL CHADWICK

✦ ✦ ✦

"Beware of the barrenness of a busy life."

CORRIE TEN BOOM

✦ ✦ ✦

"Our highest calling in life is not in
serving Jesus, but in being with Him."[6]

HOPE MACDONALD

✦ ✦ ✦

"If you sow in prayerlessness, you will reap
powerlessness, peacelessness, joylessness,
fruitlessness, and backsliddenness."

RAYMOND KWONG

"One of the greatest sins we commit against
ourselves and those around us is the sin of not
praying. . . . Our prayerless lives are the sin that
keeps the world from knowing Jesus! They are
the sin that keeps us from knowing Him!"[7]

HOPE MACDONALD

✦ ✦ ✦

"Human beings seem to have a perpetual
desire to have someone else talk to
God for them. We are content
to have the message second hand."[8]

RICHARD FOSTER

✦ ✦ ✦

"The neglect of prayer is a
grand hindrance to holiness."

JOHN WESLEY

✦ ✦ ✦

"A child of God can grieve Jesus in
no worse way than to neglect prayer."[9]

O. HALLESBY

✦ ✦ ✦

"The One who instructed us to 'be still and
know that I am God' must hurt when He
witnesses our frantic, compulsive,

agitated motions. In place of a quiet,
responsive spirit we offer Him an inner
washing machine — churning with anxiety,
clogged with too much activity,
and spilling over with resentment and
impatience. Sometimes He must watch our
convulsions with an inner sigh."[10]

CHARLES SWINDOLL

✦ ✦ ✦

"You can organize until you are exhausted;
you can plan, program, subsidize all your plans.
But if you fail to pray, it is a waste of time.
Prayer is not optional for us.
It is mandatory.
Not to pray is to disobey God."

RICHARD HALVERSON

✦ ✦ ✦

"Little prayer is characteristic of a backslidden
age and of a backslidden church.
Whenever there is little prayer in the pulpit
or the pew, spiritual bankruptcy is
imminent and inevitable."[11]

E.M. BOUNDS

✦ ✦ ✦

"We are not above all called for activity. Our life
is not just for the transformation of this world,

for if it was, we would be in a never-ending
circle. If we want to transform this world,
it is so that all may become lovers.
That is why before transforming the world we
must ourselves become lovers and open
ourselves to the experience of love, the
experience of the infinite which is very
fragile and begins in the quiet murmurings
of peace. It is here, in some moments of prayer,
or after receiving the body and blood of Jesus,
that we sense the first calls of the Spirit
to the wedding feast, to a meeting with the
spouse to the marriage of the lamb."[12]

JEAN VANIER

✦ ✦ ✦

"The minimal prayer accompanying
many projects in the church may indicate
that what is being undertaken is simply
what human beings can accomplish pretty well
by themselves."[13]

RICHARD LOVELACE

✦ ✦ ✦

"The worst sin is prayerlessness. We usually
think of murder, adultery or theft among the
worst, but the root of all sin is self-sufficiency —
independence from God. When we fail
to wait prayerfully for God's guidance and
strength, we are saying — with our action

if not our lips — that we don't need Him,
we can go it alone. The opposite of
such independence is when we acknowledge
our need of God's instruction
and supply."[14]

CHARLES HUMMEL

✦ ✦ ✦

"We need to find God, and He cannot be found
in noise and restlessness. God is the friend of
silence. See how nature — trees, flowers,
grass — grows in silence; see the stars, the
moon and sun, how they move in silence . . .
the more we receive in silent prayer,
the more we can give in our active life.
We need silence to be able to touch souls.
The essential thing is not what we say,
but what God says to us and through us.
All our words will be useless
unless they come from within —
words which do not give the light of Christ
increase the darkness."

MOTHER TERESA

✦ ✦ ✦

"We feel honestly the pull of many obligations
and try to fulfill them all. And we are unhappy,
uneasy, strained, oppressed,
and fearful we shall be shallow. . . .
We have hints that there is a way of life

vastly richer and deeper than all this
hurried existence, a life of unhurried
serenity and peace and power.
If only we could slip over into that Center!
. . . We have seen and known some people
who have found this deep Center of living,
where the fretful calls of life are integrated,
where No as well as Yes
can be said with confidence."

THOMAS KELLY

✦ ✦ ✦

"If we could take account of our losses
in spiritual things as we can in our financial,
we would be startled at what losses
we are suffering — traceable to a lack of prayer."

HENRIETTA MEARS

✦ ✦ ✦

"Failing to pray for and with one's child
day by day may be as culpable neglect
as failing to give it material substance . . ."[15]

H. CLAY TRUMBELL

✦ ✦ ✦

"Acute desire must be present or there will be
no manifestation of Christ to His people.
He waits to be wanted."

A.W. TOZER

"It is easy to mistake the voice of flattery
for the voice of God.
Especially if you've been busy for so long,
there hasn't been a really quiet time to hear
God speak. The voice of God is always
speaking to us, and always trying to get
our attention. But His voice is a
'still, small voice,' and we must at least
slow down in order to listen."[16]

EUGENIA PRICE

PRAYER AND STUDY

✦ ✦ ✦

" 'But what about you?' He asked.
'Who do you say I am?'
Simon Peter answered, 'You are the
Christ, the Son of the living God.'
Jesus replied, 'Blessed are you, Si-
mon son of Jonah, for this was not
revealed to you by man, but by My
Father in heaven.' "

Matthew 16:15-17

"It will be vain for me to stock my library,
or organize societies, or project schemes,
if I neglect the culture of myself;
for books, and agencies, and systems,
are only remotely the instruments of my
holy calling; my own spirit, soul and body
are my nearest machinery for sacred service;
my spiritual faculties, and my inner life,
are my battle axe and weapons of war."

CHARLES H. SPURGEON

✦ ✦ ✦

"The closet is the heart's study."[1]

E.M. BOUNDS

✦ ✦ ✦

"We think that we are 20th and 21st century
people, nonetheless, we have hints that
one can receive directions
as clear as those given Ananias. . . .
Rise and go to the street called Straight."[2]

ELIZABETH O'CONNOR

✦ ✦ ✦

"That conversation (prayer) when it is truly
conversation, makes an indelible impression
on our minds, and our consciousness of Him
remains vivid as we go our way."[3]

DALLAS WILLARD

"He who has prayed well has studied well."

MARTIN LUTHER

✦ ✦ ✦

"In the morning I was more engaged in
preparing the head than the heart.
This has been frequently my error, and I
have always felt the evil of it,
especially in prayer.
Reform it then, O Lord!
Enlarge my heart and I shall preach!"

ROBERT MURRAY MCCHEYNE

✦ ✦ ✦

"All our libraries and studies are
mere emptiness compared with our closets."

C.H. SPURGEON

✦ ✦ ✦

"Give yourself to prayer, and get your texts,
your thoughts, your words from God. Luther
spent his best three hours in prayer."

ROBERT MURRAY MCCHEYNE

✦ ✦ ✦

"I have been driven many times to my knees
by the overwhelming conviction
that I had nowhere else to go.

My own wisdom, and that of all about me,
seemed insufficient for the day."

ABRAHAM LINCOLN

✦ ✦ ✦

"By one hour's intimate access to the throne of
grace, where the Lord causes His glory to pass
before the soul that seeks Him,
you may acquire more true spiritual knowledge
and comfort than by a day's or a week's
converse with the best of men,
or the most studious perusal of many folios."

JOHN NEWTON

✦ ✦ ✦

"Thought is not only brightened and clarified
in prayer, but thought is born in prayer.
We can learn more in an hour praying,
when praying indeed,
than from many hours in the study."[4]

E.M. BOUNDS

✦ ✦ ✦

"Be not forgetful of prayer. Every time you pray,
if your prayer is sincere, there will be new
feeling and new meaning in it, which will
give you fresh courage, and you will
understand that prayer is an education."

FYODOR DOSTOYEVSKI

"Like art, like music, like so many other
disciplines, prayer can only be appreciated
when you actually spend time in it.
Spending time with the Master will elevate
your thinking. The more you pray,
the more will be revealed. You will
understand. You will smile and nod your head
as you identify with others who fight long
battles and find great joy on their knees."

JONI EARECKSON TADA

✦ ✦ ✦

"Let every student be plainly instructed
and earnestly pressed to consider well
the main end of his life and studies is
to know God and Jesus Christ
which is eternal life, and therefore to lay
Christ in the bottom as the only foundation
of all sound knowledge and learning
and seeing the Lord only giveth wisdom, let
everyone seriously set himself to prayer
in secret to seek it of Him."

**MOTTO OF HARVARD UNIVERSITY,
1636**

PRAYER AND PURITY

✦ ✦ ✦

"If I had cherished sin in my heart,
the Lord would not have listened."

Psalm 66:18

"If Christians spent as much time praying
as they do grumbling, they would soon
have nothing to grumble about."

ANONYMOUS

✦ ✦ ✦

"Prayer — secret, fervent, believing prayer —
lies at the root
of all personal godliness."

WILLIAM CAREY

✦ ✦ ✦

"Prayer requires that we deal with God —
this God who is determined on nothing
less than the total renovation
of our lives. We would rather have
a religious bull session."

EUGENE H. PETERSON

✦ ✦ ✦

"Prayer will make a man cease from sin,
or sin will entice a man to cease from prayer."

JOHN BUNYAN

✦ ✦ ✦

"He who has learned to pray has learned the
greatest secret of a holy and happy life."

WILLIAM LAW

"There are two main pitfalls on the road to
mastery of the art of prayer. If a person
gets what he asks for, his humility is in
danger. If he fails to get what he asks for,
he is apt to lose his confidence.
Indeed, no matter whether prayer seems
to be succeeding or failing, humility
and confidence are two virtues
which are absolutely essential."

TRAPPIST MONK

✦ ✦ ✦

"Petitions that are less pure
can only be purified by petition."[1]

P.T. FORSYTH

✦ ✦ ✦

"When we discern that people are not going on
spiritually and allow the discernment to turn to
criticism, we block our way to God. God never
gives us discernment in order that we may
criticize, but that we may intercede."[2]

OSWALD CHAMBERS

✦ ✦ ✦

"Intercessory prayer is the purifying bath
into which the individual and the
fellowship must enter every day."

DIETRICH BONHOEFFER

"When we become too glib in prayer
we are most surely talking to ourselves."

A.W. TOZER

✦ ✦ ✦

"Prayer is the act by which the community
of faith surrenders itself, puts aside
all other concerns, and comes before
God Himself. It brings us, inevitably,
as Archbishop William Temple once wrote,
to 'the nourishment of mind with His truth;
the purifying of imagination by His beauty;
the opening of the heart to His love;
the surrender of will to His purpose —
and all of this gathered up in adoration,
the most selfless emotion of which our nature
is capable and therefore the chief remedy
for all that self-centeredness
which is our original sin
and the source of all actual sin.' "[3]

CHARLES COLSON

✦ ✦ ✦

"To confess your sins to God is not
to tell Him anything He doesn't know.
Until you confess them, however,
they are the abyss between you.
When you confess them, they become
the bridge."[4]

FREDERICK BUECHNER

"We may know for certain that we shall be heard, not because we use many words, but on account of purity in our hearts and our tears of sorrow. Our prayer, therefore, should be short and pure, unless by some inspiration of divine grace it be prolonged."[5]

BENEDICT OF NURSIA

+ + +

"Until known sin is judged and renounced, we pray and plead in vain."[6]

J. OSWALD SANDERS

+ + +

"God welcomes us into His presence, accepting us no matter how 'disfigured or deformed' we are. But when we come before Him in worship, we need to make certain that we have been washed in Jesus' blood and our hearts are clean, harboring no blemish or pride or defect of impurity."[7]

JONI EARECKSON TADA

+ + +

"Intercession is not an escape from reality. Our communication with God must be rooted in the truth — the eternal truth of His holy standards and the awful truth about

American society as God sees it.
The intercessor experiences the broken heart
of God through the indwelling presence
of the Holy Spirit.
The intercessor also identifies with the
sin of the people, because the intercessor
has personally contributed to God's grief."[8]

JOHN DAWSON

✦ ✦ ✦

"My biggest problem is not demons.
I am my biggest problem. It is only when
God has cleansed my own wicked heart
that participation in the redeeming work
of intercession becomes possible.
It is then that the power to change
history is released through prayer."[9]

JOHN DAWSON

PRAYER AND UNITY

✦ ✦ ✦

"Again, I tell you that if two of you on earth agree about anything you ask for, it will be done for you by My Father in heaven."

Matthew 18:19

"What we cannot obtain by solitary prayer
we may by social . . .
because where our individual strength fails,
there union and accord are effectual."

CHRYSOSTOM

✦ ✦ ✦

"Nothing tends more to cement
the hearts of Christians than
praying together. Never do they love
one another so well as when
they witness the outpouring
of each other's hearts in prayer."

CHARLES FINNEY

✦ ✦ ✦

"The life of prayer
shapes the unity of Christian morality."

CARL F.H. HENRY

✦ ✦ ✦

"Jesus knew and spoke about
the added power that comes when
several are praying together.
It is a most glorious experience
of spiritual power, and of
fellowship together."[1]

SAM SHOEMAKER

"Disunity is a major hindrance to much prayer,
and the history of revival in the church
proves that deep, pervading unity in the Spirit
can lead to spiritual refreshing
and blessing."[2]

WESLEY DUEWEL

✦ ✦ ✦

"You have need not only for secret solitary, but
also of public united prayer. And He gives us a
very special promise for the united prayer of
two or three who agree in what they ask. . . . It
is in the union and fellowship of believers that
the Spirit can manifest His full power."[3]

ANDREW MURRAY

✦ ✦ ✦

"No soldier entering battle array prays
for himself alone but for his
fellow soldiers also. They form *one army*."

HENRIETTA MEARS

PRAYER AND SPIRIT

✦ ✦ ✦

"And pray in the Spirit on all oc-
casions with all kinds of prayers
and requests. With this in mind, be
alert and always keep on praying
for all the saints."

Ephesians 6:18

"Love of prayer is
one of the marks of the Spirit."

ANDREW MURRAY

♦ ♦ ♦

"Acknowledge you can't really pray
without the direction and energy
of the Holy Spirit. Ask God
to utterly control you by His Spirit,
receive by faith that He does, and thank Him."

JOY DAWSON

♦ ♦ ♦

"We wish to pray in the Spirit and
at the same time walk after the flesh,
and this is impossible."[1]

ANDREW MURRAY

♦ ♦ ♦

"If the skeleton and outline of our prayers be
by habit, almost a form, let us strive that
the clothing and filling up of our prayers
be as far as possible of the Spirit."

BISHOP J.C. RYLE

♦ ♦ ♦

"This is what the Scripture means when it says
that the Holy Spirit prays in us and for us, that

Christ prays for us, that we can pray aright
to God only in the name of Jesus Christ."

DIETRICH BONHOEFFER

✦ ✦ ✦

"If it becomes difficult for you to pray,
then offer this little prayer,
'Lord, teach me to pray!'
There is nothing that He,
the Spirit of prayer,
would rather do."[2]

O. HALLESBY

✦ ✦ ✦

"The whole secret of prayer
is found in those words,
'in the Spirit.' "[3]

R.A. TORREY

✦ ✦ ✦

"Only the omnipotent Holy Spirit,
applying the fruits of the finished work
of Christ through a church constantly
awakened through prayer, can deliver the lost
from the power of Satan."

**INTERNATIONAL PRAYER ASSEMBLY,
"CALL TO PRAYER"
SEOUL, KOREA, 1984**

"The Holy Spirit is the Spirit of prayer. He prays
directly, speaking with the Father and the Son.
He also prays indirectly, praying through you,
the believer. . . . To be filled with the Spirit is to
be filled with the Spirit of intercession."[4]

WESLEY DUEWEL

❖ ❖ ❖

"Unquestionably, all of us need massive help
with praying aright. So set is our flesh against
praying at all that the Helper's first task
is to create in us even the basic desire to pray.
He is the One who also spotlights for us
the prayer-need or topic for prayer
by creating a 'concern' within us."[5]

CATHERINE MARSHALL

❖ ❖ ❖

"Teach this simple experience, this prayer
of the heart. Don't teach methods;
don't teach some lofty way to pray.
Teach the prayer of God's Spirit,
not of man's invention."[6]

MADAME GUYON

❖ ❖ ❖

"God Himself, who dwells within us in
the person of the Holy Spirit, intercedes
for us in our weakness. Not with

flowery or powerful words, but with groans
that words cannot express. How empowering
in our weakest moments, when we don't know
how to express our overwhelming needs,
to cling to the words of God."[7]

SUE RICHARDS

✦ ✦ ✦

"Unless the Holy Spirit is sighed for,
cried for, prayed for,
don't assume that He's present in our
organization, in our theology,
even in our ordinances."

JOHN CALVIN

PRAYER AND COMBAT

✦ ✦ ✦

"He replied, 'This kind can come
out only by prayer.'"

Mark 9:29

"Prayer is the power that
wields the weapon of the Word."[1]

JOHN PIPER

✦ ✦ ✦

"To clasp the hands in prayer
is the beginning of an uprising
against the disorder of the world."

KARL BARTH

✦ ✦ ✦

"We should not pray for God to be on our side,
but pray that we may be on God's side."

BILLY GRAHAM

✦ ✦ ✦

"We must learn to pray far more
for spiritual victory than
for protection from battle wounds. . . .
This triumph is not deliverance from,
but victory in trial,
and that not intermittent
but perpetual."

AMY CARMICHAEL

✦ ✦ ✦

"We have so many battles going on
in America today that we should be

a people of prayer.
Our government needs prayer.
Our leaders need prayer.
Our schools need prayer.
Our youth need our prayers.
Our families need prayer."[2]

BILLY GRAHAM

✦ ✦ ✦

"Prayer is the very sword of the saints."

FRANCIS THOMPSON

✦ ✦ ✦

"If you cannot win the battle over Satan in prayer, you cannot win it in the ministry."

DAVID Y. CHO

✦ ✦ ✦

"Prayer is an act of violence."[3]

JACK HAYFORD

✦ ✦ ✦

"Prayer is not primarily
God's way of getting things done.
It is God's way of giving the church
'on the job' training in overcoming
the forces hostile to God."[4]

PAUL BILLHEIMER

"The first and decisive battle in conjunction
with prayer is the conflict which arises
when we are to make arrangements
to be alone with God every day."

O. HALLESBY

✦ ✦ ✦

"Prayer is striking the winning blow
at the concealed enemy.
Service is gathering up the results of
that blow among the (people)
we see and touch."[5]

S.D. GORDON

✦ ✦ ✦

"To have prayed well is to have fought well."[6]

E.M. BOUNDS

✦ ✦ ✦

"The enemy uses all his power to lead the
Christian, and above all the minister,
to neglect prayer."[7]

ANDREW MURRAY

✦ ✦ ✦

"Pray often, for prayer is a shield to the soul,
a sacrifice to God, and a scourge to Satan."

JOHN BUNYAN

"Prayer is warfare.
Just getting to prayer
is half the battle;
staying there is the other half."

ANONYMOUS

✦ ✦ ✦

"This is the place of prayer —
on the battlefield of the world.
It is a wartime walkie-talkie
for spiritual warfare, not a domestic intercom
to increase the comforts
of the saints."[8]

JOHN PIPER

✦ ✦ ✦

"The one concern of the devil is
to keep Christians from praying.
He fears nothing from prayerless studies,
prayerless work and prayerless religion.
He laughs at our toil, mocks at our wisdom,
but trembles when we pray."

SAMUEL CHADWICK

✦ ✦ ✦

"The Devil trembles when he sees,
God's weakest child upon his knees."

ANONYMOUS

"How now does Satan hinder prayer?
By temptation to postpone or curtail it
by bringing in wandering thoughts
and all sorts of distractions
through unbelief and hopelessness."[9]

ANDREW MURRAY

✦ ✦ ✦

"When the Church shuts herself up to the power
of the inner chamber, and the soldiers of the
Lord have received on their knees 'power from
on high,' then the powers of darkness shall be
shaken and souls will be delivered."[10]

ANDREW MURRAY

✦ ✦ ✦

"Prayer is our means of involving the
omnipotent God of the universe
in our personal battle with Satan."[11]

EVELYN CHRISTENSON

✦ ✦ ✦

"We know that our defense lies in prayer alone.
We are too weak to resist the Devil and his
servants. Let us hold fast
to the weapons of the Christian. . . .
Our enemies may mock at us, but we shall
defy them and the Devil
if we continue stedfast in prayer."

MARTIN LUTHER

"If you do not know that life is war,
you will not know what prayer is for."

JOHN PIPER

✦ ✦ ✦

"In its simplest meaning
prayer has to do with spirit conflict."[12]

S.D. GORDON

✦ ✦ ✦

"Our most strategic confrontation is not,
first of all, with Satan. Our first confrontation
is with the Lord of Glory Himself,
as we humble ourselves under
His mighty hand."[13]

DAVID BRYANT

✦ ✦ ✦

"Pray or be a prey — a prey to fears,
to futilities, to ineffectiveness."[14]

E. STANLEY JONES

✦ ✦ ✦

"When a Christian shuns fellowship with other
Christians, the devil smiles. When he stops
reading the Bible, the devil laughs. When he
stops praying, the devil shouts for joy."[15]

CORRIE TEN BOOM

"The secret prayer chamber is a
bloody battleground. Here violent and
decisive battles are fought out."[16]

O. HALLESBY

+ + +

"When God's house on earth is a house
of prayer, then God's house in heaven is busy
and all-potent in its plans and movements;
then His earthly armies are clothed
with the triumphs and spoils of victory
and His enemies defeated on every hand."[17]

E.M. BOUNDS

+ + +

"The enemy of our souls is painfully aware
of the destructive force of even our
dullest and weakest prayers and will go
to any length to block them."[18]

RICHARD LOVELACE

+ + +

"What prayer does is to enable us,
not to find a way round the hard thing,
but to go straight through it,
not to avoid it but to accept it and overcome it.
Prayer is not evasion; prayer is conquest."[19]

WILLIAM BARCLAY

"Whoever wrestles with God in prayer
puts his whole life at stake.
Otherwise it would not be a genuine combat, or
indeed it would not be a combat with God."[20]

JACQUES ELLUL

✦ ✦ ✦

"A 'prayer warrior' is a person who is convinced
that God is omnipotent — that God has the
power to do anything, to change anyone and to
intervene in any circumstance. A person who
truly believes this refuses to doubt God."[21]

BILL HYBELS

✦ ✦ ✦

"To pray with all your heart and strength —
that is the last, the greatest of the
Christian's warfare on earth."

THE KNEELING CHRISTIAN

✦ ✦ ✦

"Prayer is the shout of the fighting believer."

CHARLES SPURGEON

✦ ✦ ✦

"Prayer is a labour above all labours
since he who prays must wage a mighty warfare
against the doubt and murmuring excited

by the faintheartedness and unworthiness
we feel within us."

MARTIN LUTHER

✦ ✦ ✦

"If you can beat the devil in the matter
of regular daily prayer, you can beat him anywhere. If he can beat you there,
he can possibly beat you anywhere."

PAUL RADER

✦ ✦ ✦

"Much of our praying is just asking God to bless
some folks that are ill and to keep us plugging
along. But prayer is not merely prattle:
it is warfare."

ALAN REDPATH

✦ ✦ ✦

"Neglect of prayer is a guarantee
that we will not be victors."

RICHARD OWEN ROBERTS

✦ ✦ ✦

"The armour is for the battle of prayer.
The armour is not to fight in,
but to shield us while we pray.
Prayer is the battle."

OSWALD CHAMBERS

"Lose the importunity of prayer, reduce it to
soliloquy, or even to colloquy, with God,
lose the real conflict of will and will,
lose the habit of wrestling and the hope of
prevailing with God,
make it mere walking with God in friendly talk;
and, precious as it is, yet you tend to lose the
reality of prayer at last.
In principle you make it mere conversation
instead of the soul's great action.
You lose the food of character, the renewal
of will. You may have beautiful prayers —
but as ineffectual as beauty so often is,
and as fleeting."

P.T. FORSYTH

PRAYER AND REVIVAL

✦ ✦ ✦

"If My *people, who are called by*
My *name, will humble themselves*
and pray and seek My *face and*
turn from their wicked ways, then
will I hear from heaven and will
forgive their sin and will heal their
land."

2 Chronicles 7:14

"Envision this:
You let God's heart for the lost
become your heart for the lost.
You and your friends begin a city wide
prayer movement. Then comes revival
in the local churches, followed by
an awakening among non-Christians,
reformation of society, and
a new expression of world mission."

JOHN DAWSON

✦ ✦ ✦

"There has never been a spiritual awakening
in any country or locality
that did not begin in united prayer."

A.T. PIERSON

✦ ✦ ✦

"History is full of exciting results
as God has worked through concerted,
united, sustained prayer."

J. EDWIN ORR

✦ ✦ ✦

"An Humble Attempt to Promote
Explicit Agreement and Visible Union
of God's People through the World
in Extraordinary Prayer, for the Revival
of Religion and the Advancement

of Christ's Kingdom on Earth,
Pursuant to Scripture Promises and
Prophecies, Concerning the Last Time."
**THE TITLE OF A WORK PUBLISHED
IN 1748 BY JONATHAN EDWARDS**

✦ ✦ ✦

"There is a lot of praying *about* revival, but that
will not bring it about. Jesus did not pray about
things, He brought them about by prayer."[1]
ARMIN GESSWEIN

✦ ✦ ✦

"There have been revivals without
much preaching; but there has never been a
mighty revival without mighty prayer."
R.A. TORREY

✦ ✦ ✦

"Every new Pentecost has had its
preparatory period of supplication."[2]
A.T. PIERSON

✦ ✦ ✦

"If prayer is a fireplace,
and people set themselves to praying,
then the fire can't be far behind."
ANONYMOUS

"Dr. A.T. Pierson said it well,
when he said that no Revival has ever come
except by that kind (Upper Room) of praying,
and (he continued) no Revival has continued
beyond the continuation of the same kind
of praying. It's like a fire — what gets
it started is what it takes
to keep it burning."[3]

ARMIN GESSWEIN

✦ ✦ ✦

"Without a doubt, the major opportunity
before us is the potential of a historic revival
akin to the first great awakening. . . .
The encouraging 'sign' of an impending
awakening is the grass-roots prayer movement
God is raising up through this nation."[4]

PAUL CEDAR

✦ ✦ ✦

"After studying prayer and spiritual awakenings
for 60 years I've reached this conclusion —
whenever God is ready to do something new
with His people, He always sets them praying."

DR. J. EDWIN ORR

✦ ✦ ✦

"Never before in living memory has prayer
been rising so rapidly on the agenda

of Christian leaders across our nation.
Is the great revival on the way?"[5]

C. PETER WAGNER

✦ ✦ ✦

"William Carey and a small praying band in
Kettering, England, prayed monthly for nearly
eight years before mighty revival came.
William Wilberforce was used of God to bring
moral and spiritual awakening to England.
He had the backing of a group
in his church that covenanted together
to pray three hours a day."[6]

WESLEY DUEWEL

✦ ✦ ✦

"When people sense the Lord is near,
they also want to talk with Him.
Revival and prayer always go together."[7]

DAVID MAINS

✦ ✦ ✦

"A revival may be expected when Christians
have a spirit of prayer for a revival;
that is, when they pray as if their hearts were set
upon a revival. Sometimes Christians are not
engaged in prayer for a revival not even when
they are warm in prayer. Their minds are
upon something else — the salvation of

the heathen and the like — and not for revival
among themselves."[8]

CHARLES FINNEY

✦ ✦ ✦

"Moody attributed his marvelous success
to the prayers of an obscure and
almost unknown invalid woman! And truly
the invalid saints of England could bring
about a speedy revival by their prayers.
Oh, that all the 'shut-ins' would speak out!"

THE KNEELING CHRISTIAN

✦ ✦ ✦

"Here is a tremendous truth,
God's very revelation on the subject
of church revival.
Like priest, like people.
The congregation seldom rises above
the level of the minister.
If he is a man of faith and love,
the congregation will become that way.
If he is a man of prayer,
he will build a praying people."[9]

ARMIN GESSWEIN

✦ ✦ ✦

"Once again, today God has raised up
a multitude who are willing to pay the price

both by praying and by preaching,
so that the church might encounter the
full panorama of who Christ is.
And to the degree that they succeed —
to the degree God restores in us an 'abounding
hope by the power of the Holy Spirit,'
and does so for the church worldwide —
to that degree we will experience
a true world revival."[10]

DAVID BRYANT

✦ ✦ ✦

"When prayers and strong pleas for revival are
made to God both day and night;
when the children of God find they can
no longer tolerate the absence of revival
blessings; when extraordinary seeking of an
extraordinary outpouring becomes
extraordinarily earnest; and when the
burden of prayer for revival becomes
almost unbearable, then let praying hearts
take courage, for the Spirit of God who is
the spirit of revival has brought
His people to this place for a purpose."

RICHARD OWEN ROBERTS

✦ ✦ ✦

"It's not like an earth quake.
It's more like being lifted by the tide,
a surging tide of God's grace.

Across the world, the new decade is marked
by the emergence of citywide prayer meetings.
Some of the largest pastoral prayer meetings in
United States history have recently taken place.
. . . What is God up to?
We can only wonder at His tactics,
but His motives are clear enough. He loves us.
He has not abandoned our generation.
He governs in the affairs of people and nations,
and He is setting the stage for harvest."[11]

JOHN DAWSON

PRAYER AND MISSION

✦ ✦ ✦

"Then He said to His disciples,
'The harvest is plentiful but the
workers are few. Ask the Lord of the
harvest, therefore, to send out
workers into His harvest field.' "

Matthew 9:37-38

"Many people grieve because they have been
denied service on the Mission Field
or in some other chosen endeavor.
But through faithful intercession they
may accomplish as much and reap as full a
reward as though they had been
on the mission field in person."

PAUL BILLHEIMER

✦ ✦ ✦

"Every step in the progress of missions
is directly traceable to prayer."

A.T. PIERSON

✦ ✦ ✦

"In due time the weeping intercessor
will become the rejoicing winner of souls."

C.H. SPURGEON

✦ ✦ ✦

"The Christian is a holy rebel loose in the world
with access to the throne of God."

A.W. TOZER

✦ ✦ ✦

"A movement of prayer for the world must
first target on our own spiritual blindness.
Once Christ is revealed in the midst of His

Church, we will be spiritually propelled
into the urgent ministry given us
to extend His kingdom among the nations."[1]

DAVID BRYANT

✦ ✦ ✦

"The number and efficiency of the laborers
in God's vineyard in all lands
is dependent on the men of prayer."[2]

E.M. BOUNDS

✦ ✦ ✦

"In this supernatural cause (world missions),
which rests on a supernatural charter and is led
by an omnipotent leader with all His power
pledged to support it, a neglect of prayer is
actually a denial that God is leading. Neglect of
prayer is a willful limitation of success."[3]

ROBERT SPEER

✦ ✦ ✦

"God's whole vision for the whole world
can only be fulfilled through the
whole Body of Christ. Therefore, the
whole Body must pursue that vision together.
And, the most strategic way to pursue it
is through a movement of united prayer for
spiritual awakening and world evangelization."

DAVID BRYANT

"Don't ever underestimate the mission
of prayer. Through it we can love
any of the world's unreached peoples,
even at the ends of the earth."

DAVID BRYANT

✦ ✦ ✦

"The frontline in world evangelization
is the Word of God and prayer."

ERIC ALEXANDER

✦ ✦ ✦

"How to multiply the number of Christians who,
with clear, unshakeable faith in the character
of God, will wield this force of intercession —
that is the supreme question of
foreign missions."[4]

ANDREW MURRAY

✦ ✦ ✦

"To make intercession for men is the most powerful and practical way in which
we can express our love for them."

JOHN CALVIN

✦ ✦ ✦

"It is not age, experience, talent,
or material wealth that makes the difference

in the destiny of men and nations.
Prayer alone will change the world."

DICK EASTMAN

✦ ✦ ✦

"The greatest impact any of us can have
on Christ's global cause is to be involved
in consistent prayer for the whole world
and to teach other Christians
how to pray this way."[5]

DAVID BRYANT

✦ ✦ ✦

"We have become in missions so wrapped up in
technology and methodology that we have
forgotten that missions is number one
the releasing of divine dynamics. Reaching
the unreached will, first of all, mean for us
not only to lay hold of it in faith,
but to develop thousands and thousands of
prayer cells in America and elsewhere
that will commit themselves wholeheartedly
to prayer until the victory will be won.
We need spiritual mobilization."

GEORGE PETERS

✦ ✦ ✦

"Undoubtedly the small quantity of intelligent
intercessory prayer in most twentieth-century

congregations is part of the short circuiting
of missionary consciousness among the laity.
The establishment of the kingdom of God
is an elusive task; we cannot even see
what it involves in our vicinity
without specific prayer, and we certainly
will have little urgency to carry it out
unless we are praying."[6]

RICHARD LOVELACE

✦ ✦ ✦

"World evangelization is to be numbered
among the primary goals in prayer,
since the proclaiming of the gospel
is what gives glory to God."[7]

DONALD BLOESCH

PRAYER AND PROMISE

✦ ✦ ✦

"For no matter how many promises God has made, they are 'Yes' in Christ. And so through Him the 'Amen' is spoken by us to the glory of God."

2 Corinthians 1:20

"Tarry at a promise
and God will meet you there."

D.L. MOODY

✦ ✦ ✦

"Learn to plead the promises of God."[1]

ARMIN GESSWEIN

✦ ✦ ✦

"The promises of God give size,
shape and success to our prayers."[2]

ARMIN GESSWEIN

✦ ✦ ✦

"Here (in the Psalter) we learn,
first what prayer means. It means praying according to the Word of God, on the basis
of promises."[3]

DIETRICH BONHOEFFER

✦ ✦ ✦

"Without the promise, prayer is
eccentric and baseless.
Without prayer, the promise is dim,
voiceless, shadowy, and impersonal.
The promise makes prayer
dauntless and irresistible."[4]

E.M. BOUNDS

"Every promise of Scripture is a writing of God,
which may be pledged before Him
with this reasonable request:
'Do as Thou hast said.' "

C.H. SPURGEON

✦ ✦ ✦

"Prayer is simply asking God to do for us
what He has promised to do if we ask Him."[5]

E.M. BOUNDS

✦ ✦ ✦

"We should take the new covenant promises
of God and plead with God to bring them to
pass in our children and our neighbors and
on all the mission fields of the world. . . .
When we believe in the sovereignty of God —
in the right and power of God to elect and
then bring hardened sinners to faith
and salvation — then we will be able to pray
with no inconsistency, and with great biblical
promises for the conversion of the lost."[6]

JOHN PIPER

PRAYER AND LISTENING

✦ ✦ ✦

"Guard your steps when you go to the house of God. Go near to listen rather than to offer the sacrifice of fools, who do not know that they do wrong."

Ecclesiastes 5:1

"Prayer at its highest is
a two-way conversation
and for me the most important
is listening to God's replies."

FRANK LAUBACH

✦ ✦ ✦

"We must hear, know and obey the
will of God before we pray
into the lives of others."

RICHARD FOSTER

✦ ✦ ✦

"God is always speaking;
He's always doing something.
Prayer is to enter into that activity.
Prayer in its most basic sense is just
getting into an attitude of saying,
'Lord, what are you saying to me?'"

HENRI NOUWEN

✦ ✦ ✦

"Instead of each of us making
a prayer speech to Him, let's talk
things over with Him, back and forth,
including Him in it, as we do
when we have a conversation."[1]

ROSALIND RINKER

✦ ✦ ✦

"Best friends are always good listeners.
If we truly desire to be friends
with the Lord, we must learn the secret
of listening."[2]

DICK EASTMAN

✦ ✦ ✦

"A man prayed, and at first
he thought that prayer was talking.
But he became more and more quiet
until in the end he realized
that prayer is listening."

SÖREN KIERKEGAARD

✦ ✦ ✦

"You can't build a relationship on
one-way speeches. You need frequent,
sustained, intimate contact between
two persons, both of whom speak
and both of whom listen. . . .
Listening to God speak to us through His Holy
Spirit is not only normal; it is essential."[3]

BILL HYBELS

✦ ✦ ✦

"Prayer reminds us of our constant need for
God and reassures us of His presence with us.
In prayer we don't tell God what to do;
we find out what He wants us to do."

DAVID HUBBARD

"If God were to call, would He get a busy signal?"

ANONYMOUS

✦ ✦ ✦

"God sometimes seems to speak to us most intimately when He catches us, as it were, off our guard. Our preparations to receive Him sometimes have the opposite effect. Doesn't Charles Williams say somewhere that 'the altar most often be built in one place in order that the fire from heaven may descend somewhere else'?"[4]

C.S. LEWIS

✦ ✦ ✦

"Prayer starts with God. Our desire to pray is the result of His call to prayer. He has something to say. Our responsibility is to listen to what He wants to give us for our problems and potential."[5]

LLOYD JOHN OGILVIE

✦ ✦ ✦

"Rest, Rest, Rest in God's love. The only work you are required now to do is to give your most intense attention to His still, small voice within."

MADAME JEANNE GUYON

"It is not that I will not hear God,
but I am not devoted in the right place.
I am devoted to things, to service,
to convictions, and God may say what He likes
but I do not hear Him.
The child attitude is always,
'Speak, Lord, for Thy servant heareth.' "[6]

OSWALD CHAMBERS

✦ ✦ ✦

"You need not cry very loud;
He is nearer to us than we think."

BROTHER LAWRENCE

✦ ✦ ✦

"We are besieged by words in our society.
Billboards blaze them into our minds as we go by.
Headlines scream from the newspapers.
Regular prayer builds into our lives
those experiences of silence and concentration
when the still, small voice of our Saviour
can cut through life's howl
and speak His words of peace and joy."[7]

DAVID HUBBARD

✦ ✦ ✦

"Wait on the Lord for insight. Don't rely on finite
reasoning or human cunning. Spiritual battles
are won by following revelation given by the

Holy Spirit. If we listen to God with childlike dependency, He will guide us into victory."[8]

JOHN DAWSON

✦ ✦ ✦

"The great adventure of listening to God can be scary sometimes. Often God tells me to call or write to someone, or apologize for something I've done, or give away a possession, or start a new ministry. . . ."[9]

BILL HYBELS

✦ ✦ ✦

"To me, this is real prayer — expecting God to talk to me through His Word as I talk to Him."[10]

BILL BRIGHT

✦ ✦ ✦

"It is not enough for God to speak to us: He must grant us the power to hear and understand. . . . From our side, prayer begins in listening and seeking to hear the Word of God. It consists in a response to the voice of God speaking within the depths of our soul. Before there can be meaningful conversation with God we must take time to wait on the Lord in silent expectation."[11]

DONALD BLOESCH

"However difficult it may sound,
the hearing really precedes the asking.
It is the basis of it. It makes it real asking,
the asking of Christian prayer."[12]

KARL BARTH

✦ ✦ ✦

"Disengagement means silence before God,
first of all. It is a time of heavenly discussion
during which we listen more than we speak.
And silence demands solitude.
Does it impress you, as it does me,
that these are two matters which our world
is substantially ignorant of
and often seems to resist?"[13]

GAIL MACDONALD

✦ ✦ ✦

"We must take time to listen to God.
We must remove all the clutter and static
that keeps us from hearing His voice to us. . . .
As God's people are humbled before Him,
silence not only means that we have a
sense of awe, but also a spirit of readiness
to respond to the Lord no matter what. . . ."[14]

DAVID BRYANT

PRAYER AND QUIETNESS

✦ ✦ ✦

"Come with Me by yourselves to a quiet place."

Mark 6:31

"Before we are ready to start our intercessory
prayers, we need to wait before God
until we know we have established
communication with Him.
This is a time of silence when we are
shutting out every other thought
and distraction around us.
This is not talking to God,
just a complete mental drawing to Him;
and then, as He promised,
He will draw nigh to us."[1]

EVELYN CHRISTENSON

✦ ✦ ✦

"Only in quiet waters does God cast His anchor.
God only draws near to a soul that enters
quietness, a soul whose thoughts and feelings
have been stilled."[2]

BASILEA SCHLINK

✦ ✦ ✦

"Finding a quiet time: With young children in the
home there will be few uninterrupted stretches
of time. So watch for free minutes,
chinks of time throughout the day to pray.
The question really is, how much do you *want*
to pray? Claim this promise for the
quiet heart: 'For God is not the author
of confusion, but of peace. . . !' (1 Cor. 14:33)"[3]

CATHERINE MARSHALL

"Through the Prayer of Rest God places His
children in the eye of the storm. When all
around us is chaos and confusion,
deep within we know stability and serenity.
In the midst of intense personal struggle
we are still and relaxed. While a thousand frustra-
tions seek to distract us, we remain focused and
attentive. This is the fruit of the Prayer of Rest."[4]

RICHARD FOSTER

✦ ✦ ✦

"Do not be afraid of silence in your prayer time.
It may be that you are meant to listen, not to
speak. So wait before the Lord. Wait in stillness.
Wait as David waited when he 'sat before the
Lord.' And in that stillness,
assurance will come to you.
You will know that you are heard;
you will know that your Lord ponders
the voice of your humble desires;
you will hear quiet words spoken
to you yourself, perhaps to your
grateful surprise and refreshment."[5]

AMY CARMICHAEL

✦ ✦ ✦

"We seldom read of God's appearing by Himself
or His angels to any of His prophets or saints in
a throng but frequently when they are alone."

RICHARD BAXTER

"We have to pitch our tents where we shall always have quiet times with God, however noisy our times with the world may be."

OSWALD CHAMBERS

PRAYER AND PREACHING

✦ ✦ ✦

"Finally, brothers, pray for us that
the message of the Lord may spread
rapidly and be honored, just as it
was with you."

2 Thessalonians 3:1

"It is sad that most ministers have
more hours of training in how to talk
and be with people than how to talk
and be with God."

HENRI NOUWEN

✦ ✦ ✦

"Prayerless pews make powerless pulpits."

ROBERT C. SAVAGE

✦ ✦ ✦

"God has made the spread of His fame hang
on the preaching of His Word, and He has made
the preaching of His Word hang on the prayers
of the saints . . . the triumph of the Word
will not come without prayer."[1]

JOHN PIPER

✦ ✦ ✦

"If some Christians that have been complaining
of their ministers had said and acted less
before men and had applied themselves
with all their might to cry out to God
for their ministers — had as it were,
risen and stormed heaven with their humble,
fervent, and incessant prayers for them —
they would have been much more in
the way of success."

JONATHAN EDWARDS

"I am very sensitive and know whether
you are praying for me. If one of you
lets me down, I feel it. When you are praying
for me, I feel a strange power. When everyone
in a congregation prays intensely
while the pastor is preaching,
a miracle happens."

FRANK LAUBACH

✦ ✦ ✦

"Talking to men for God is a great thing,
but talking to God for men
is greater still."[2]

E.M. BOUNDS

✦ ✦ ✦

"None are so able to plead with men
as those who have been wrestling with God
on their behalf."

C.H. SPURGEON

✦ ✦ ✦

"The truth is employed to influence men,
and prayer to move God . . . truth by itself
will never produce the effect without
the Spirit of God, and the Spirit is given
in answer to prayer."[3]

CHARLES FINNEY

"Preaching that kills is prayerless preaching.
Without prayer, the preacher creates death and
not life. The preacher who is feeble in prayer
is feeble in life-giving forces."[4]

E.M. BOUNDS

✦ ✦ ✦

"In the morning I was more engaged in
preparing the head than the heart.
This has been frequently my error, and I
have always felt the evil of it, especially
in prayer. Reform it, then, O Lord!
Enlarge my heart, and I shall preach."

ROBERT MURRAY MCCHEYNE

✦ ✦ ✦

"Want of private devotional reading and
shortness of prayer through incessant
sermon-making had produced much
strangeness between God and my soul."

HENRY MARTYN

PRAYER AND RELATIONSHIPS

✦ ✦ ✦

"And when you stand praying, if you hold anything against anyone, forgive him, so that your Father in heaven may forgive you your sins."

Mark 11:25

"Husbands, in the same way be considerate as you live with your wives, and treat them with respect as the weaker partner and as heirs with you of the gracious gift of life, so that nothing will hinder your prayers."

1 Peter 3:7

"Intercessory prayer might be defined
as loving our neighbor on our knees."

CHARLES H. BRENT

✦ ✦ ✦

"If we do not love one another we certainly shall
not have much power with God in prayer."

D.L. MOODY

✦ ✦ ✦

"Criticism of others nails them to the past.
Prayer for them releases them into the future."

FRANK LAUBACH

✦ ✦ ✦

"A Christian fellowship lives and exists
by the intercession of its members
for one another, or it collapses.
I can no longer condemn or hate a
brother for whom I pray,
no matter how much trouble he causes me."[1]

DIETRICH BONHOEFFER

✦ ✦ ✦

"Last week while praying I suddenly discovered
that I had really forgiven someone I have been
trying to forgive for over thirty years."[2]

C.S. LEWIS

"The first followers of Christ seem to support all their love, and to maintain all their intercourse and correspondence, by mutual prayers for one another. This was the ancient friendship of Christians, uniting and cementing their hearts."

WILLIAM LAW

✦ ✦ ✦

"A loving spirit is a condition of believing prayer. We cannot be wrong with man and right with God."

THE KNEELING CHRISTIAN

✦ ✦ ✦

"There is nothing that makes us love a man so much as praying for him."

WILLIAM LAW

PRAYER AND PRAISE

✦ ✦ ✦

"He said to them, 'When you pray,
say: "Father, hallowed be Your
name, Your kingdom come." ' "

Luke 11:2

"With the earliest birds I will make one
more singer in the great concert-hall of God.
I will not want more rest, or a longer time
to myself to consider all my troubles,
I will give my best time, the first hour
of the day, to the praise of my God."[1]

CHARLES H. SPURGEON

✦ ✦ ✦

"The worth and excellency of a soul is
to be measured by the object of its love."

HENRY SEAGAL

✦ ✦ ✦

"The only way to fly is to praise;
it's the way to remain airborne."[2]

JACK HAYFORD

✦ ✦ ✦

"Solomon prevailed much with God in prayer
at the dedication of the temple
but it was the voice of praise which brought
down the glory and filled the house."[3]

D.L. MOODY

✦ ✦ ✦

"Since adoration brings man into immediate
and direct contact with God,

✦ ✦ ✦

in the role of servant to master,
or the created to the Creator,
it is foundational to all other kinds of prayer."[4]

HAROLD LINDSELL

✦ ✦ ✦

"God manifests His loving presence
in the praise-saturated chamber of prayer.
Adoration is the antidote to the
poison of Satanic oppression."[5]

DICK EASTMAN

✦ ✦ ✦

"Worship is the bottom line
of our communication with God."[6]

MELVA WICKMAN

✦ ✦ ✦

"Only a sovereign God can inspire prayer,
and only a sovereign God can answer prayer . . .
real prayer begins
and ends with God enthroned."[7]

RALPH HERRING

✦ ✦ ✦

"Prayer of praise is devoted directly to God
for His own sake apart from anything we may
or may not have received from Him."[8]

HENRI J.M. NOUWEN

"The secret of answered prayer is
faith without doubt. And the secret of
faith without doubt is praise, triumphant praise,
continuous praise, praise that is
a way of life."[9]

PAUL BILLHEIMER

✦ ✦ ✦

"Thanksgiving means thanking God for
all the good gifts which He has given to us.
One of the great dangers of life is that
we should take things for granted just
because they come to us regularly
and every day."[10]

WILLIAM BARCLAY

✦ ✦ ✦

"Is it a struggle for you to pray?
Do your prayers seem lifeless to you?
There is a way to revive your prayer life.
Begin to give thanks for everything in your
life for which you owe God thanks.
And if you have any needs that you
have asked God to supply,
in accordance with His promise,
give thanks in advance that He will
hear your prayers. . . . Such thanksgiving
will cheer your heart, bring new life
to your prayers and draw down God's grace."[11]

BASILEA SCHLINK

"There is real danger of worshipping prayer
instead of praying because we worship."[12]

OSWALD CHAMBERS

✦ ✦ ✦

"You awaken us to delight in your praise;
for you have made us for yourself,
and our hearts are restless
until they rest in you."

AUGUSTINE

✦ ✦ ✦

"A Christian is more music
When he prays,
Than spheres, or angel's praises be,
In panegyric alleluias."

JOHN DONNE

PRAYER AND PAIN

✦ ✦ ✦

"We know that the whole creation
has been groaning as in the pains
of childbirth right up to the present
time. . . . In the same way, the
Spirit helps us in our weakness.
We do not know what we ought to
pray, but the Spirit Himself intercedes for us with groans that words
cannot express."

Romans 8:22, 26

"Groanings which cannot be uttered are often
prayers which cannot be refused."

CHARLES H. SPURGEON

✦ ✦ ✦

"I have never come to a time of prayer
but that it has been with a struggle."

HORATIO BONAR

✦ ✦ ✦

"This period of devotions must contain a period
of pain. It is not God's intention that we should
writhe under it, or linger in it.
But specific and sincere confession of our
own sin is no joyous exercise."

E.M. BLAIKLOCK

✦ ✦ ✦

"All vital praying makes a drain on man's
vitality. True intercession is
a sacrifice, a bleeding sacrifice."

J.H. JOWETT

✦ ✦ ✦

"Abstraction is an enemy to prayer.
Beautiful ideas are an enemy to prayer.
Fine thoughts are an enemy to prayer.
Authentic prayer begins when we

stub our toes on a rock,
get drenched in a rainstorm,
get slapped in the face
by the enemy."

EUGENE PETERSON

✦ ✦ ✦

"Spiritual birth, like physical birth,
is always accompanied by labor pains."

ANONYMOUS

✦ ✦ ✦

"O my God, deep calls unto deep.
The deep of my profound misery
calls to the deep of Your profound mercy."[1]

BERNARD OF CLAIRVAUX

✦ ✦ ✦

"To be faced with what one writer called
the 'withering winds of God's
hiddenness' does not mean that
God is displeased with you,
or that you are insensitive to the
work of God's Spirit, or that you have
committed some horrendous offense
against heaven, or anything.
Darkness is a part of our experience of
prayer. It is to be expected, even embraced."[2]

RICHARD J. FOSTER

"I found that when some Russians who were
in great tribulation and persecution heard
that we were willing to pray for them,
they never said, 'Pray that God will
stop this persecution.' They said,
'pray that God will give us the strength
to suffer for Him.' "[3]

CORRIE TEN BOOM

✦ ✦ ✦

"Let your suffering be borne for God, suffer
with submission and patience and suffer in
unison with Jesus Christ and you will be
offering a most excellent prayer."

JEAN-NICHOLAS GROU

✦ ✦ ✦

"If the spirit groans in intercession,
do not be afraid of the agony of prayer.
There are blessings of the kingdom
that are only yielded to the
violence of the vehement soul."[4]

SAMUEL CHADWICK

✦ ✦ ✦

"Jesus is the supreme model of a person
devoted to prayer. He was constantly in
an attitude of prayer, and never more
urgently than in the face of suffering."[5]

BILLY GRAHAM

"Persecution, whether it is physical,
social, or mental, is one of the worst types
of pain, but those who persecute us
are to be the objects
of our prayers."[6]

BILLY GRAHAM

✦ ✦ ✦

"At times, God calls us to weep.
This is His call to empathy,
to vicarious intercessory identification
with others. At such times, we must be sure
to pray 'us' prayers and not 'them' prayers.
We must identify with those in need,
rather than condemn and accuse."[7]

WESLEY DUEWEL

✦ ✦ ✦

"Just as the contractions of a woman's uterus
herald the beginning of labor,
there are times when God's Spirit stirs
our souls to seasons of intense travail.
We must travail in prayer
until God's purposes are birthed."[8]

JOHN DAWSON

✦ ✦ ✦

"There is no birth without travail."

ANONYMOUS

"Prayer and pains through faith in Jesus Christ
will do anything."

JOHN ELIOT

✦ ✦ ✦

"We stop praying when our hearts are sorrowful.
This is the Enemy's objective. He knows that
prayer is our sole help in extreme
distress. . . . Therefore, do not listen to the
voice of the Enemy when you are in suffering.
Rather, listen to the voice of God. Heed His
challenge. Even though you may not feel like it,
start to pray — and prayer will help you . . . for it
will bring you into deeper communion with
God — the greatest joy of all."[9]

BASILEA SCHLINK

✦ ✦ ✦

"Remember, it is prayer based on His agony,
not on our agony."[10]

OSWALD CHAMBERS

PRAYER AND PERSEVERANCE

✦ ✦ ✦

"Then Jesus told His disciples a parable to show them that they should always pray and not give up. . . . 'And will not God bring about justice for His chosen ones, who cry out to Him day and night? Will He keep putting them off?' "

Luke 18:1, 7

"Units of prayer combined like drops of water,
can make an ocean that defies resistance."

E.M. BOUNDS

✦ ✦ ✦

"Many a man asks in April a gift of divine fruit
that will be ripe only in June."

ANONYMOUS

✦ ✦ ✦

"George Mueller prayed fifty-two years
for an unsaved loved one, but it wasn't
until some time after he died that his
loved one came to know Jesus Christ as Savior.
I believe our prayers go right on
living and working even after we die."[1]

HOPE MACDONALD

✦ ✦ ✦

"To pray correctly means to
keep on praying until revival comes."

JOHN HYDE

✦ ✦ ✦

"According to Jesus, by far the most important
thing about praying is to keep at it."[2]

FREDERICK BUECHNER

"Of all the mysteries of the prayer world,
the need of persevering prayer is one of the
greatest. . . . Just as the ploughman
has to take his ten thousand steps, and
sow his ten thousand seeds, each one a
preparation for the final harvest, so there is
a need-be for oft-repeated persevering
prayer, all working out some desired blessing."[3]

ANDREW MURRAY

✦ ✦ ✦

"It is not enough to begin to pray, nor to pray
aright; nor is it enough to continue for a time
to pray; but we must patiently, believingly,
continue in prayer until we obtain an answer."

GEORGE MUELLER

✦ ✦ ✦

"The Scriptures say, 'Pray without ceasing'
(1 Thessalonians 5:17, KJV). This should be the
motto of every true follower of Jesus. No matter
how dark and hopeless a situation might seem,
never stop praying. It's not only to resolve our
problems that we should pray, but to share in
the strength of God's friendship."[4]

BILLY GRAHAM

✦ ✦ ✦

"Continual prayer will be appropriate —
yes, required — in many cases.

Large issues have long-range consequences
that may require a lot of time to work out."[5]

JACK HAYFORD

✦ ✦ ✦

"If you would never cease to pray,
never cease to long for it.
The continuance of your longing is
the continuance of your prayer."

AUGUSTINE

✦ ✦ ✦

"To think there's always going to be a quick
solution or even a satisfactory-to-us answer
is a faulty expectation. Sometimes answers to
prayer lie dormant, being fertilized by
unceasing prayer. When the seed finally
germinates, rapid growth can take place."[6]

EDITH SCHAEFFER

✦ ✦ ✦

"Whatever it takes for you to own the doctrine
of God's omnipotence, do it. Until you own it,
you will be a faint-hearted pray-er.
You'll make a few wishes on your knees,
but you won't be able to persevere in prayer
until you know in your heart that God is able."[7]

BILL HYBELS

PRAYER AND SCRIPTURE

✦ ✦ ✦

"If you remain in Me and My words remain in you, ask whatever you wish, and it will be given you."

John 15:7

"We should never read the Bible
without praying, and we should never pray
without reading the Bible."[1]

ARMIN GESSWEIN

✦ ✦ ✦

"The Bible is not just the answer Book.
The Bible is also the asking Book.
Answering and asking are
both God's department."[2]

ARMIN GESSWEIN

✦ ✦ ✦

"The Word of God is the fulcrum
upon which the lever of prayer is placed,
and by which things are
mightily moved."

E.M. BOUNDS

✦ ✦ ✦

"Little of the Word with little prayer
is death to the spiritual life. Much of the Word
with little prayer gives a sickly life.
Much prayer with little of the Word gives
more life, but without stedfastness. A full
measure of the Word and prayer each day gives
a healthy and powerful life."[3]

ANDREW MURRAY

"By bringing God's Word directly into our
praying, we are bringing God's power
directly into our praying."[4]

DICK EASTMAN

✦ ✦ ✦

"God's Word is known at the throne. Use it every
time you pray. It is your prayer language."[5]

ARMIN GESSWEIN

✦ ✦ ✦

"The most promising method of prayer is to
allow oneself to be guided by the word of the
Scriptures, to pray on the basis of a word of
Scripture. In this way we shall not become
the victims of our own emptiness."[6]

DIETRICH BONHOEFFER

✦ ✦ ✦

"God's listening to our voice depends
upon our listening to His voice."[7]

ANDREW MURRAY

PRAYER AND GRACE

✦ ✦ ✦

"Who has ever given to God, that God should repay him? For from Him and through Him and to Him are all things. To Him be the glory forever! Amen."

Romans 11:35-36

"Prayer is a grace, a gift from God."[1]

KARL BARTH

✦ ✦ ✦

"If God did not hear sinners,
in vain would the publican have said,
'God be merciful to me a sinner.' "

AUGUSTINE

✦ ✦ ✦

"The truth of the matter is, we all come with a
tangled mess of motives — altruistic and selfish,
merciful and hateful, loving and bitter.
Frankly, this side of eternity we will
never unravel the good from the bad,
the pure from the impure.
But what I have come to see is that God is
big enough to receive us with all our mixture.
We do not have to be bright or pure,
or filled with faith, or anything.
That is what grace means, and not only
are we saved by grace, we live by it as well.
And we pray by it."[2]

RICHARD FOSTER

✦ ✦ ✦

"Just as faith is a gift of God,
so prayer is a gift of God;
praying people are a gift of God;

and a movement of united prayer for revival
and missions is a gift of God.
It all begins and ends with Christ."[3]

DAVID BRYANT

✦ ✦ ✦

"The efficacy of prayer does not depend upon
my ability as a 'pray-er' or on the intensity of my
praying. It does depend upon my trust. But even
my trust, my faith, Is not strictly my own doing.
'It is the gift of God — not by works, so that no
one can boast' (Ephesians 2:8-9)."[4]

ROGER PALMS

✦ ✦ ✦

"All of God's answering our prayers
is upon the basis of God's dealings
with us as forgiven sinners,
and God cannot deal with us as
forgiven sinners while we are not
forgiving those who have wronged us."

R.A. TORREY

✦ ✦ ✦

"We pursue God because, and only because,
He has first put an urge within us that
spurs us to the pursuit.
'No man can come to Me,' said our Lord,
'except the Father which hath sent Me draw

him,' and it is by this very prevenient
drawing that God takes from us every vestige
of credit for the act of coming."[5]

A.W. TOZER

✦ ✦ ✦

"True contemplation is not a psychological trick
but a theological grace."

THOMAS MERTON

✦ ✦ ✦

"Jesus' intercession ensures that
when we approach His throne in our weakness
and inadequacy, we find it to be a
'throne of grace' where we 'receive mercy
and find grace to help us in our time of
need' (Hebrews 4:16). No spiritual benefit of
any kind comes to any child of God apart from
the mediatorial intercession of Jesus the Lord."[6]

J.I. PACKER

✦ ✦ ✦

"God is always previous."[7]

A.W. TOZER

✦ ✦ ✦

"God loves His church too much to leave us
in our unrevived condition . . . God knows

that the church is in such a condition
that our healing and restoration, and our
re-deployment in the mission of Christ, is way
beyond our ability to accomplish ourselves.
He must bring us to repentance. He must
reverse the predispositions within us. He must
raise us up, set us free, and send us forth."[8]

DAVID BRYANT

✦ ✦ ✦

"Because of our natural aversion to prayer . . .
God Himself must stir up the work of prayer
in us. Just as faith is a gift of God, so prayer is a
gift of God. Therefore, praying people are a gift
from God, and movements of prayer are a gift
from God. And if God is giving this gift, He will
not fail to answer the prayers that He Himself
has actually stirred up to begin with."[9]

DAVID BRYANT

✦ ✦ ✦

"The lesson that has become more basic
to my thinking than any other is that
prayer begins and ends with God."[10]

JOHN WHITE

✦ ✦ ✦

"I do not see prayer as man acting upon God,
but God acting upon man.

It is Jesus expressing His own ministry of
intercession through those He has drawn
and energized by His Spirit.
It is Jesus the Discipler of nations,
Jesus the Lord of the harvest,
Jesus the Captain of the heavenly host,
Jesus the Head of the Church . . .
He gives us daily direction and we trust
that eternal destiny is being worked out
through our simple response to His grace."[11]

JOHN DAWSON

PRAYER IN SECRET

✦ ✦ ✦

"But when you pray, do not be like the hypocrites, for they love to pray standing in the synagogues and on the street corners to be seen by men. I tell you the truth, they have received their reward in full. But when you pray, go into your room, close the door and pray to your Father, who is unseen. Then your Father, who sees what is done in secret, will reward you."

Matthew 6:5-6

"The secret of all failure is
failure in secret prayer."

THE KNEELING CHRISTIAN

✦ ✦ ✦

"The secret ministry of prayer
is the secret of ministry."[1]

ARMIN GESSWEIN

✦ ✦ ✦

"I have found that the more I do in secret
prayer, the more I have delighted to do, and the
more I have enjoyed in the spirit of prayer."

DAVID BRAINERD

✦ ✦ ✦

"God knows the weakness of the human heart
towards pride. If we speak of what God has
revealed and done in intercession,
it may lead to committing this sin.
God shares His secrets with those
who are able to keep them."

JOHN DAWSON

✦ ✦ ✦

"God makes all His best people in loneliness.
Do you know what the secret of praying is?
Praying in secret."[2]

LEONARD RAVENHILL

"The first thing the Lord teaches His disciples
is that they must have a secret place
for prayer; every one must have a solitary spot
where he can be alone with his God.
Every teacher must have a schoolroom."[3]

ANDREW MURRAY

✦ ✦ ✦

"Secrecy helps us get rid
of hindrances to praying with our spirit.
For instance, in our room with the door shut,
we are not so likely to strut and pose
and pretend as we are when another human being is present. We know that we cannot
deceive God. Transparent honesty
before Him is easier for us
in isolation."[4]

CATHERINE MARSHALL

✦ ✦ ✦

"You will find in your 'closet of prayer'
what you frequently lose when you are
out in the world. The more you visit it,
the more you will want to return.
If you are faithful to your secret place,
it will become your closest friend
and bring you much comfort.
The tears shed there bring cleansing."

THOMAS à KEMPIS

"Let every student be plainly instructed
and earnestly pressed to consider well
the main end of his life and studies
is to know God and Jesus Christ which is
eternal life, and therefore to lay Christ
in the bottom as the only foundation
of all sound knowledge and learning
and seeing the Lord only giveth wisdom,
let everyone seriously set himself to
prayer in secret to seek it of Him."

**MOTTO OF HARVARD UNIVERSITY,
1636**

PRAYER IN PRACTICE

✦ ✦ ✦

"They devoted themselves to the apostles' teaching and to the fellowship, to the breaking of bread and to prayer."

Acts 2:42

"Learn to pray by praying."[1]

ARMIN GESSWEIN

✦ ✦ ✦

"Certain requirements must be met if the
art of prayer is to be acquired.
In the main there are two —
practice and perseverance."

O. HALLESBY

✦ ✦ ✦

"The great people of the earth today are
the people who pray — not those who
talk about prayer; nor those who say
they believe in prayer; nor those who
can explain about prayer;
but those who take time to pray."[2]

S.D. GORDON

✦ ✦ ✦

"There is no way to learn to pray
except by praying."

J. OSWALD SANDERS

✦ ✦ ✦

"The art of prayer must be learned,
for reservoirs of power are at our disposal
if we can learn this art. 'If we learn it' —

that is the rub. People expect results
without any practice of the art."[3]

E. STANLEY JONES

✦ ✦ ✦

"It was said of the late C.H. Spurgeon
that he glided from laughter to prayer
with the naturalness of one who lived in
both elements. With him the habit of
prayer was free and unfettered."[4]

E.M. BOUNDS

✦ ✦ ✦

"Understanding the principles of a subject,
knowing the rules of a game, or
reading a handbook about some craft
does not perfect a person in a trade or sport.
There is no substitute for doing the thing.
The same is true of prayer.
Practice perfects, matures, and develops."[5]

JACK HAYFORD

✦ ✦ ✦

"One can pray inwardly at any time
and anywhere — in a subway or on an athletic
field. But one prays best either alone
or with understanding friends.
To avoid neglecting to pray, it is best
to have a time-habit and a place-habit.

This is so important that it is worth
great effort, in spite of the hurry of
life and our lack of privacy."
GEORGIA HARKNESS

PRAYER IN PARTNERSHIP

✦ ✦ ✦

"I *looked for a man among them who would build up the wall and stand before Me in the gap on behalf of the land so I would not have to destroy it, but I found none."*

Ezekiel 22:30

"For it is God who works in you to will and to act according to His good purpose."

Philipplans 2:13

"Never sinner prays truly
without Christ praying
at the same time."

C.H. SPURGEON

✦ ✦ ✦

"It is not our prayer which moves the Lord Jesus.
It is Jesus who moves us to pray."

O. HALLESBY

✦ ✦ ✦

"How seldom it is realized that
prayer covers the whole divine mystery
of men's partnership with the Trinity
in working out the counsel
of His will and grace."[1]

ANDREW MURRAY

✦ ✦ ✦

"Without God, we cannot.
Without us, God will not."

AUGUSTINE

✦ ✦ ✦

"We pursue God because and only because
He has first put an urge within us
that spurs us on to the pursuit."[2]

A.W. TOZER

"God always hears
the prayers of His Son,
and if the Son of God is formed in me
the Father will always hear my prayers."[3]

OSWALD CHAMBERS

✦ ✦ ✦

"Since Jesus ever lives to intercede,
any time you pray — day or night —
Jesus is already interceding.
Every time you go to prayer
you can be Jesus' prayer partner."[4]

WESLEY DUEWEL

✦ ✦ ✦

"When I learn what intercession is,
and how to respond to the Holy Spirit's
prodding to do it, I am moving into partnership
with the Father in the highest sense."[5]

JACK HAYFORD

✦ ✦ ✦

"We move into the deepest kind
of interior prayer in order that
we may be found by God,
recognized by the Lord of our lives,
and loved into being."[6]

MADELEINE L'ENGLE

"Prayer is a dialogue between two people
who love each other—
God and man."

ANONYMOUS

✦ ✦ ✦

"A real man or woman of prayer . . . should be a
live wire, a link between God's grace and the
world that needs it. In so far as you have given
your lives to God, you have offered yourselves,
without conditions, as transmitters
of His saving and enabling love."[7]

EVELYN UNDERHILL

✦ ✦ ✦

"Why cannot an omnipotent God, knowing our
needs, supply them without waiting for our
prayers? He could, of course, but that is not His
plan for His children on earth.
Instead, He has dared to arrange it
so that He is actually dependent upon us
in the sense of prayers being necessary
and all-important to the
carrying out of His will on earth."[8]

CATHERINE MARSHALL

✦ ✦ ✦

"Yes, we need Divine help for prayer—
and we have it!

How the whole Trinity delights in prayer!
God the Father listens:
the Holy Spirit dictates:
the eternal Son presents the petition
and Himself intercedes;
and so the answer comes down."

THE KNEELING CHRISTIAN

✦ ✦ ✦

"Jesus teaches us to pray together in
dialogue prayer in order to release
God's power to bind evil and release good.
Dialogue prayer is simply conversational prayer,
two people praying back and forth. . . .
This prayer-power requires the presence of our
risen Lord and our cooperation in audible
prayer. This changes us and the situations for
which we pray."[9]

ROSALIND RINKER

✦ ✦ ✦

"To pray is a supernatural way of getting to
know a supernatural God. When we pray, God
makes us His partners! He chooses us to
become part of His ministry here on earth."[10]

ROSALIND RINKER

✦ ✦ ✦

"When we speak to God it is really
the God who lives in us speaking through us

to Himself. . . . The dialogue of grace
is really the monologue of the
divine nature in self-communing love."[11]

P.T. FORSYTH

✦ ✦ ✦

"God makes us covenant partners in the
working out of His purposes in the world,
and yet we are not equal partners.
God is the senior partner and must therefore
be approached in awe and reverence."[12]

DONALD BLOESCH

✦ ✦ ✦

"An intercessor means one who is in such vital
contact with God and with his fellow men that
he is like a live wire closing the gap between the
saving power of God and the sinful men who
have been cut off from that power."

HANNAH HURNARD

✦ ✦ ✦

"True prayers are like carrier pigeons: from
heaven they came, they are only going home."

CHARLES SPURGEON

PRAYER UNANSWERED

✦ ✦ ✦

"How long, O Lord, must I call for help, but You do not listen?"

Habakkuk 1:2

"When you ask, you do not receive, because you ask with wrong motives, that you may spend what you get on your pleasures."

James 4:3

"We shall come one day to a heaven
where we shall gratefully know that
God's great refusals were sometimes
the true answers to our truest prayer."[1]

P.T. FORSYTH

✦ ✦ ✦

"If God had granted all the silly prayers I've
made in my life, where would I be now?"[2]

C.S. LEWIS

✦ ✦ ✦

"Every war, every famine or plague,
almost every death bed, is the monument
to a petition that was not granted."[3]

C.S. LEWIS

✦ ✦ ✦

"Many times in our short sightedness we ask for
things that are not in our best interests.
At other times the answer to our prayers would
be detrimental to others, or mean the refusal of
their prayers, or both. Then there are times
when our prayers are simply self-contradictory,
a 'grant me patience' quickly kind of prayer.
And, finally, sometimes our prayers,
if answered, would do us in. We are simply
not prepared for what we have asked."[4]

RICHARD J. FOSTER

"When prayer seems to be unanswered,
beware of trying to fix the blame on
someone else. That is always a snare of
Satan. You will find there is a reason
which is a deep instruction to you,
not to anyone else. . . . We are not here to
prove God answers prayer; we are here
to be living monuments of God's grace."[5]

OSWALD CHAMBERS

✦ ✦ ✦

"God is true to His word and answers all
sincere prayers offered in the name of the
Lord Jesus Christ. His answer may be yes,
or it may be no, or it may be 'Wait.'
If it is no or 'Wait,' we cannot say that
God has not answered our prayer.
It simply means that the answer is
different from what we expected."[6]

BILLY GRAHAM

✦ ✦ ✦

"Once when I was going through a dark period
I prayed long and earnestly, but there was no
answer. I felt as though God was indifferent
and that I was all alone with my problem.
It was what some would call 'a dark night
of the soul.' I wrote my mother about the
experience, and I will never forget her reply:
'Son, there are many times when God

withdraws to test your faith. He wants you
to trust Him in the darkness. Now, Son,
reach up by faith in the fog and you will
find that His hand will be there.' "[7]

BILLY GRAHAM

✦ ✦ ✦

"When He grants our prayers,
it is because He loves us.
When He does not, it is also
because He loves us."

O. HALLESBY

✦ ✦ ✦

"When God closes a door,
He always opens a window."

MARIA VON TRAPP

✦ ✦ ✦

"If the request is wrong, God says, 'No.'
If the timing is wrong, God says, 'Slow.'
If you are wrong, God says, 'Grow.'
But if the request is right, the timing is right
and you are right, God says, 'Go!' "

ANONYMOUS

✦ ✦ ✦

"God's silences are His answers."[8]

OSWALD CHAMBERS

"Often God delays purposely,
and the delay is just as much an answer
to your prayer as is the
fulfillment when it comes."[9]

MRS. CHARLES E. COWMAN

✦ ✦ ✦

"God has not always answered my prayers.
If He had, I would have married the
wrong man — several times!"

RUTH BELL GRAHAM

PRAYER FROM GOD'S PERSPECTIVE

✦ ✦ ✦

"I *revealed* Myself *to those who did not ask for Me; I was found by those who did not seek Me. To a nation that did not call on My name, I said, 'Here am I, here am I.'*"

Isaiah 65:1

"God has always been the initiator
and man the responder."

EUGENE PETERSON

✦ ✦ ✦

"The trouble with you is this:
You have been thinking of the quiet time,
of the Bible study and prayer time
as a factor in your own spiritual progress,
but you have forgotten that this hour
means something to Me also.
Remember 'I love you.
I have redeemed you at a great cost.
I desire your fellowship.' "[1]

ROBERT BOYD MUNGER

✦ ✦ ✦

"God wants to hear our requests, for it is
His great pleasure to fulfill them."

BASILEA SCHLINK

✦ ✦ ✦

"I must believe in His infinite love,
which really longs to have communion
with me every moment and
to keep me in the enjoyment
of His fellowship."

ANDREW MURRAY

"The call to prayer is the Father's invitation
to visit with Him. This is more than
the consciousness of a great need that
often drives us to intercession.
It is the call of love to come
and fellowship."[2]

E.W. KENYON

✦ ✦ ✦

"A human king can hearken to two or three
people at one time, but he cannot hearken
to more. God is not so. For all men
may pray to Him and He hearkens
to them all simultaneously. Men's ears
become satisfied with hearing
but God's ears are never satisfied;
He is never wearied by men's prayers."

THE MIDRASH

✦ ✦ ✦

"God warms His hands at man's heart
when he prays."

JOHN MASEFIELD

✦ ✦ ✦

"You pay God a compliment by
asking great things of Him."

TERESA OF AVILA

"You know, the truth that Christ
wants my fellowship, that He loves me,
wants me to be with Him
and waits for me,
has done more to transform my quiet time
with God than any other single fact."[3]

ROBERT BOYD MUNGER

✦ ✦ ✦

"God awaits eagerly for us, His spiritual
children, to come to Him in prayer.
This is the Creator God who, in spite of
our sin and self-centeredness,
has done so much for us. As incredible as
it seems, God wants our fellowship!"[4]

BILL BRIGHT

✦ ✦ ✦

"This is the nature of the encounter, not that I
am stumbling towards the Abba Father, but that
the Abba Father is running towards me.''[5]

STEPHEN VERNEY

PRAYER AND FASTING

◆ ◆ ◆

"They said to me, 'Those who sur-
vived the exile and are back in the
province are in great trouble and
disgrace. The wall of Jerusalem is
broken down, and its gates have
been burned with fire.' When I
heard these things, I sat down and
wept. For some days I mourned
and fasted and prayed before the
God of heaven."

Nehemiah 1:3-4

I'll always remember!

"Fasting can bring break through
in the spiritual realm that
could never be had
in any other way."[1]

RICHARD FOSTER

✦ ✦ ✦

"On the basis of the record of the whole Bible,
I would say that prayer and fasting combined
constitute the strongest single weapon
that has been committed to
God's believing people."[2]

DEREK PRINCE

✦ ✦ ✦

"Fasting helps to express, to deepen, and to
confirm the resolution that we are ready to
sacrifice anything, to sacrifice ourselves
to attain what we seek for the Kingdom of God."

ANDREW MURRAY

✦ ✦ ✦

"Fasting confirms our utter dependence
upon God by finding in Him a source of
sustenance beyond food . . . fasting
unto our Lord therefore is feasting—
feasting on Him and on doing His will."[3]

DALLAS WILLARD

"Fasting is designed to make prayer mount up
on eagles' wings. . . . If the motive to fast is
proper, Heaven is ready to bend its ear to listen
when someone prays with fasting."[4]

ARTHUR WALLIS

✦ ✦ ✦

"Prayer is the one hand with which we grasp the
Invisible; fasting the other, with which we
let loose and cast away the visible."

ANDREW MURRAY

✦ ✦ ✦

"John Calvin was called an inveterate faster —
and lived to see God's power sweep Geneva.
The Moravians fasted, as did the
Hussites, Walensians, Huguenots, and Scottish
Covenanters. Except for prevailing prayer
that included fasting, we would have had
no Reformation and no great awakenings
over the centuries."[5]

WESLEY DUEWEL

✦ ✦ ✦

"The Lord Jesus fasted for forty days.
Other illustrations of Spirit-led fasting
are Elijah, Moses, David, Ezekiel,
Nehemiah and Paul.
In the Old Testament, without exception,

the saving of nations occurred as a result
of a call to fast, repent, and pray.
The exceptional measure was taken for the
exceptional emergency because
crisis calls for desperate action."[6]

DR. JOON GON KIM

✦ ✦ ✦

"Bear up the hands that hang down, by faith and
prayer; support the tottering knees.
Have you any days of fasting and prayer?
Storm the throne of grace and persevere
therein, and mercy will come down."

JOHN WESLEY

PRAYER AND HUMILITY

✦ ✦ ✦

"You say, 'I am rich; I have acquired wealth and do not need a
thing.' But you do not realize that
you are wretched, pitiful, poor,
blind and naked. I counsel you to
buy from Me gold refined in the
fire, so you can become rich; and
white clothes to wear, so you can
cover your shameful nakedness;
and salve to put on your eyes, so
you can see."

Revelation 3:17-18

"We must turn to God in complete confidence
in the hour of battle, abide strongly
in the presence of His divine majesty,
worship Him humbly, and set before Him
our woes and our weaknesses.
And thus we shall find
in Him all virtues though
we may lack them all."

BROTHER LAWRENCE

✦ ✦ ✦

"Prayer is a radical conversion of
all our mental processes because in prayer
we move away from ourselves, our worries,
preoccupations, and self-gratification —
and direct all that we recognize as ours
to God in the simple trust that through His love
all will be made new."[1]

HENRI J.M. NOUWEN

✦ ✦ ✦

"The life that intends
to be wholly obedient, wholly submissive,
wholly listening, is astonishing in
its completeness. Its joys are ravishing,
its peace profound, its humility the deepest,
its power world shaking, its love enveloping,
its simplicity that of a trusting child."[2]

THOMAS KELLY

"In Simple Prayer we bring ourselves before God
just as we are, warts and all. Like children
before a loving father, we open our hearts
and make our requests. We do not try to
sort things out, the good from the bad.
We simply and unpretentiously share
our concerns and make our petitions."[3]

RICHARD FOSTER

✦ ✦ ✦

"God gives where He finds empty hands."

AUGUSTINE

✦ ✦ ✦

"The first thing that makes a prayer acceptable
to God is the brokenness and humility of the
one who prays: 'If My people who are called by
My name *humble themselves* and pray . . . I will
hear from heaven.' . . . In other words,
what makes a heart upright and what makes
prayers pleasing to God is a felt awareness
of our tremendous need for mercy."[4]

JOHN PIPER

✦ ✦ ✦

"Admittance to the school of prayer is by an en-
trance test with only two questions. The first
one is: Are you in real need? The second is: Do
you admit that you are helpless to handle that

need? Why would God insist on helplessness as a prerequisite to answered prayer? One obvious reason is because our human helplessness is a bed-rock fact. God is a realist and insists that we be realists too. So long as we are deluding ourselves that human resources can supply our heart's desires, we are believing a lie."[5]

CATHERINE MARSHALL

✦ ✦ ✦

"Humility is the principal aid to prayer."

TERESA OF AVILA

✦ ✦ ✦

"He knows little of himself who does not know that he is wretched, and miserable, and poor, and blind, and naked; but until he begins at least to suspect a need, how can he pray?"

GEORGE MACDONALD

✦ ✦ ✦

"I always feel like a beginner in prayer."[6]

ELIZABETH LARSEN

✦ ✦ ✦

"We are never so high as when we are on our knees."

THE KNEELING CHRISTIAN

"It does not need to be a formal prayer:
the most stumbling and broken cry — a sigh,
a whisper, anything that tells the heart's
loneliness and need and penitence —
can find its way to Him."

PHILLIPS BROOKS

✦ ✦ ✦

"Prayer and helplessness are inseparable.
Only he who is helpless can truly pray.
Your helplessness is your best prayer.
It calls from your heart to the heart of
God with greater effect than all
your uttered pleas."

O. HALLESBY

✦ ✦ ✦

"The deepest prayer at its nub is a perpetual
surrender to God."[7]

THOMAS MERTON

PRAYER AND HEALING

✦ ✦ ✦

"Is any one of you sick? He should
call the elders of the church to pray
over him and anoint him with oil
in the name of the Lord. And the
prayer offered in faith will make the
sick person well; the Lord will raise
him up. If he has sinned, he will be
forgiven."

James 5:14-15

"Pure praying remedies all ills, cures all
diseases, relieves all situations,
however dire, most calamitous, most fearful
and despairing . . . no case is mortal
when Almighty God is the physician."[1]

E.M. BOUNDS

+ + +

"It is only in the cases where all therapeutics are
inapplicable or have failed, that the results of
prayer can be surely proved. The medical board
of Lourdes has rendered a great service to
science in demonstrating the reality of the cure.
Prayer has, sometimes, an explosive effect."

DR. ALEXIS CARREL

+ + +

"Normally the aid of prayer and the
aid of medicine should be pursued
at the same time and with equal vigor,
for both are gifts from God."[2]

RICHARD FOSTER

+ + +

"A doctor who sees a patient give
himself to prayer, can indeed rejoice.
The calm engendered by prayer
is a powerful aid to healing."[3]

DR. ALEXIS CARREL

Beloved, I pray . . . you may be in health. (3 John 2)
"God has no vested interests in sickness
and infirmity. We may say that it is His
general desire, as it was the apostle's for his
friend Gaius, that His people should be
in health. Exceptions to this do not negative
the general rule. If this were not the case
He would never have equipped the human body
with its own wonderful healing powers or
His Church with a healing ministry."[4]

ARTHUR WALLIS

PRAYER AND ALERTNESS

✦ ✦ ✦

"Then He returned to His disciples
and found them sleeping. 'Could
you men not keep watch with Me
for one hour?' He asked Peter.
'Watch and pray so that you will
not fall into temptation. The spirit
is willing, but the body is weak.' "

Matthew 26:40-41

"No one in his senses, if he has any power
of ordering his own day, would reserve
his chief prayers for bed time . . .
obviously the most impossible hour
for any action which needs concentration."[1]

C.S. LEWIS

✦ ✦ ✦

"Alert praying is a major component
in spiritual warfare. To be alert means
to 'sleep in the open,' ready
for battle at any moment. It is prayer
which can switch gears
at a moment's notice."[2]

GEORGE MALLONE

✦ ✦ ✦

"You must keep a look-out,
and see if God grants the blessing
when you ask Him.
People sometimes pray,
and never look to see
if the prayer is granted."[3]

CHARLES FINNEY

✦ ✦ ✦

"To pray correctly one must be mentally alert
and vigilant. Much praying is hampered
by a dull, drowsy frame of mind."[4]

CURTIS MITCHELL

"If the heart wanders or is distracted,
bring it back to the point quite gently
and replace it tenderly in its Master's presence.
And even if you did nothing during the whole
of your hour but bring your heart back and
place it again in our Lord's presence, though
it went away every time you brought it back,
your hour would be very well employed."

FRANCIS DE SALES

PRAYER AND HOPE

✦ ✦ ✦

"Now to Him who is able to do
immeasurably more than all we ask
or imagine, according to His power
that is at work within us, to Him
be glory in the church and in
Christ Jesus throughout all generations, for ever and ever! Amen."

Ephesians 3:20-21

"When you pray with hope, you turn yourself
toward a God who will bring forth His promises;
it is enough to know that He is a faithful God."[1]

HENRI J.M. NOUWEN

✦ ✦ ✦

"Nothing is ever wasted in the kingdom of God.
Not one tear, not all our pain, not the
unanswered questions or the seemingly
unanswered prayers. . . . Nothing will be wasted
if we give our lives to God. And if we are
willing to be patient until the grace of God
is made manifest, whether it takes nine years
or ninety, it will be worth the wait."[2]

REBECCA MANLEY PIPPERT

✦ ✦ ✦

"Oxygen is to fire what hope is to prayer."

ANONYMOUS

✦ ✦ ✦

"One thing you can be sure of is that down the
path you beat with even your most half-cocked
and halting prayer the God you call upon
will finally come, and even if He does not
bring you the answer you want,
He will bring you Himself. And maybe
at the secret heart of all our prayers that is
what we are really praying for."[3]

FREDERICK BUECHNER

"After you've worshiped and petitioned to the
best of your Holy-Spirit-energized ability,
rest it all with Him. The answers may not come
in the size packages you suppose, or be
delivered at the moment you have in mind.
But trust in Him. All power and glory are His.
And in freely and praisefully speaking that,
you open the door to His invitation that you
share it with Him . . . in His way, at His time."[4]

JACK HAYFORD

✦ ✦ ✦

"We remain faithful in hope.
Ultimately — even if it be after seven years —
our united appeal to the Father will
intensify and accelerate the Kingdom's coming.
The morning will dawn for our generation.
With healing power, Christ will reveal Himself
grandly in the midst of His Church before the
eyes of the nations as the hope of glory.
To that end we must struggle in prayer
with all the energy God gives us."[5]

DAVID BRYANT

✦ ✦ ✦

"If we would pray fruitfully, we ought . . . to
grasp with both hands this assurance of
obtaining what we ask, which the Lord enjoins
with His own voice, and all the saints teach
by their example. For only that prayer is

acceptable to God which is . . . grounded
in unshaken assurance of hope."

JOHN CALVIN

✦ ✦ ✦

"As we focus our prayers today on world revival,
we pray not simply with a spirit of hopefulness.
We pray with a living Hope — and that hope is
Christ Himself. We pray with our eyes toward
that final Revival, when there will be a
simultaneous realization of God's promises of
all that His grace longs to do, and of all that
His interventions in every other revival
have actually set in motion."[6]

DAVID BRYANT

✦ ✦ ✦

"The Christian can face the future with a holy
optimism knowing that Jesus Christ is victor
over all the powers of death, hell, and
darkness. . . . To pray for the coming of the
kingdom is to pray for the manifestation of
deepening fulfillment of the victory of
Jesus Christ in the life of the church
and the world today
as well as at the end of the age."[7]

DONALD BLOESCH

NOTES

✦ ✦ ✦

INTRODUCTION
1. Bill Hybels, *Too Busy Not to Pray* (Downers Grove, Ill.: InterVarsity Press, 1988), 7.

Chapter 1 PRAYER'S PRIORITY
1. William Law, *A Serious Call to a Devout and Holy Life* (Philadelphia: Westminster Press, 1955), 91.
2. Cited by Becky Tirabassi, *Releasing God's Power* (Nashville: Thomas Nelson, 1990), 43.
3. Cited by E.M. Bounds, *Power through Prayer* (Chicago: Moody Press, 1979), 105. Used by permission.
4. From a message given at a Minister's Revival Prayer Fellowship Conference in 1983, directed by Armin Gesswein.
5. Richard Foster, *Prayer: Finding the Heart's True Home* (San Francisco: Harper & Row, 1992), 6.
6. Dick Eastman, *The Hour That Changes the World* (Grand Rapids: Baker Book House, 1978), 151.

7. From a message given at First Covenant Church, Oakland, California in 1989.

8. Billy Graham, "Prayer" tract (Minneapolis: BGEA, n.d.), 1.

9. E. Stanley Jones, *Abundant Living* (Nashville: Abingdon Press, 1942 copyright by Whitmore and Stone; Copyright © renewal 1970 by E. Stanley Jones. Used by special permission of the publisher, Abingdon Press), 58.

10. Corrie ten Boom, *Each New Day* (Old Tappan, N.J.: Fleming H. Revell, 1977), July 19 entry.

11. Ibid., August 14 entry.

12. Paul Billheimer, *Destined for the Throne* (Fort Washington, Pa.: Christian Literature Crusade, 1975), 18.

13. Andrew Murray, *State of the Church* (Fort Washington, Pa.: Christian Literature Crusade, 1983), 138.

14. Oswald Chambers, *My Utmost for His Highest* (New York: Dodd, Mead & Co., 1961), 147.

15. E.M. Bounds, *Purpose in Prayer* (Chicago: Moody Press, 1979), 9. Used by permission.

16. Jack Hayford, *Prayer Is Invading the Impossible* (Plainfield, N.J.: Logos, 1977), 125.

17. Gordon MacDonald, *Ordering Your Private World* (Nashville: Thomas Nelson, 1984), 146.

18. Marjorie Holmes, *How Can I Find God?* (Garden City, N.Y.: Doubleday Company, Inc., 1975), 122.

19. Evelyn Christenson, *What Happens When Women Pray* (Wheaton, Ill.: Victor Books, 1975), 19.

20. *The Kneeling Christian* by an Unknown Christian. Copyright © 1971 by Zondervan Publishing House. Used by permission of Zondervan Publishing House, 144.

21. Karen Burton Mains, *With My Whole Heart* (Portland, Ore.: Multnomah Press, 1987).

Chapter 2 PRAYER'S PURPOSE
1. Bill Hybels, *Too Busy Not to Pray* (Downers Grove, Ill.: InterVarsity Press, 1988), 7.
2. Mother Teresa, *A Gift for God* (New York: Harper & Row Publishers, 1975), 84.
3. E.M. Bounds, *Purpose in Prayer* (Chicago: Moody Press, 1979), 79.
4. Westminster Shorter Catechism Q 98. Cited in Philip Schaff, ed., *The Creeds of Christendom* (New York: Harper, 1919, Vol. 3), 698.

Chapter 3 PRAYER POWER
1. Billy Graham, *Hope for the Troubled Heart* (Minneapolis: Grayson, 1991), 151.
2. From a talk given at a School of Prayer, June 1992.
3. From a talk given at a prayer conference at First Covenant Church, Oakland, California, 1989.
4. Jack Hayford, *Prayer Is Invading the Impossible* (Plainfield, N.J.: Logos, 1979), 65–66.
5. Charles Spurgeon, *Twelve Sermons on Prayer* (New York: Fleming Revell, 1890), 31.
6. E.M. Bounds, *Power through Prayer* (Chicago: Moody Press, 1979), 83.
7. O. Hallesby, *Prayer* (Minneapolis: Augsburg, 1931), 117.
8. Wesley Duewel, *Mighty Prevailing Prayer* (Grand Rapids: Zondervan, 1990), 119. Used by permission.

9. Graham, *Hope for the Troubled Heart*, 153–54.

10. Sam Shoemaker, *Extraordinary Living for Ordinary Men* (Grand Rapids: Zondervan, 1965), 114.

11. E.M. Bounds, *Purpose in Prayer* (Chicago: Moody Press, 1979), 39.

12. Hayford, *Prayer Is Invading the Impossible*, 29.

13. Charles Colson, *The Body* (Dallas: Word, 1992), 143.

14. Richard Lovelace, *Dynamics of Spiritual Life* (Downers Grove, Ill.: InterVarsity Press, 1980), 160.

15. Evelyn Christenson, *What Happens When Women Pray* (Wheaton, Ill.: Victor Books, 1975), 45.

16. Corrie ten Boom, *Each New Day* (Old Tappan, N.J.: Fleming H. Revell, 1977), 1334.

17. Karl Barth, *Prayer*, Trans. by Sara F. Terrien (Philadelphia: Westminster Press, 1952), 63.

18. Armin Gesswein, "Fire in the Church," *Decision Magazine*, March 1964, 4, © 1964 Billy Graham Evangelistic Association, used by permission, all rights reserved.

19. Martin Luther, *Luther's Works*, vol. 6, ed. J. Pelikan (St. Louis: Concordia, 1970), 159.

20. Cited by Draper, *Draper's Book of Quotations for the Christian World* (Wheaton, Ill.: Tyndale House, 1992), 489.

21. Shared with compiler in personal conversation.

Chapter 4 PRAYER PRIORITIES

1. John Allan Lavender, *Why Prayers Are Unanswered* (Valley Forge, Pa.: Judson Press, 1967), 18. Used by permission of Judson Press.

2. Aquinas, *On Prayer and the Contemplative Life*, 99.

3. C.S. Lewis, *Letters to Malcolm: Chiefly on Prayer* (New York: Harcourt, Brace & Company, 1963), 19.

4. Oswald Chambers, *My Utmost for His Highest* (New York: Dodd, Mead & Co., 1961), 124.

5. Sam Shoemaker, *Extraordinary Living for Ordinary Men* (Grand Rapids: Zondervan, 1965), 114.

6. Charles Colson, *The Body* (Dallas: Word, 1992), 142.

7. P.T. Forsyth, *The Soul of Prayer*, 64.

8. Ibid., 79.

9. O. Hallesby, *Prayer* (Minneapolis: Augsburg, 1931), 128.

10. Basilea Schlink, *More Precious Than Gold* (Carol Stream, Ill.: Creation House, 1978), 204.

Chapter 5 PRAYER AND WORK

1. Richard Foster, *Celebration of Discipline* (New York: Harper & Row, 1978), 40.

2. Dallas Willard, *The Spirit of the Disciplines* (San Francisco: Harper & Row, 1988), 185.

3. Karl Barth, *Prayer and Preaching* (London: SCM Press LTD, 1964).

4. Richard C. Halverson, *Intercessors for America Newsletter*, Vol. 13, No. 4, April 1986.

5. Thomas Kelly, *A Testament of Devotion* (New York: Harper & Row, 1941), 35.

6. Foster, *Celebration of Discipline*, 39.

7. From a message given at First Covenant Church, Oakland, California, 1989.

8. Corrie ten Boom, *Each New Day* (Old Tappan, N.J.: Fleming H. Revell, 1977), July 20 entry.

9. C.H. Spurgeon, *Twelve Sermons on Prayer* (New York: Fleming H. Revell, 1890), 150.

10. Brother Lawrence, *Practice of the Presence of God* (Old Tappan, N.J.: Fleming H. Revell, 1956), 60.

11. Watchman Nee, *The Prayer Ministry of the Church* (New York: Christian Fellowship Publications, 1973), 27–28.

12. Dietrich Bonhoeffer, *Life Together* (New York: Harper & Row, 1954), 71.

13. Bryan Jeffery Leech, from an unpublished article, *The Lord's Prayer*, December 1992.

14. Dag Hammarskjold, *Markings*, trans. Leif Sjoberg and W.H. Auden (New York: Alfred A. Knopf, Inc., 1964), 156.

15. Meister Eckhart, *Meister Eckhart*, ed. and trans. by Raymond Blakeny (New York: Harper, 1941), 111.

16. J. Oswald Sanders, *Prayer Power Unlimited* (Chicago: Moody Press, 1977), 152. Used by permission.

17. Oswald Chambers, *If Ye Shall Ask* (Toronto: McClelland & Stewart Limited, 1938), 100.

18. C.S. Lewis, *Letters to Malcolm Chiefly on Prayer* (New York: Harcourt, Brace & Company, 1963), 66.

Chapter 6 PRAYER AND FAITH

1. Billy Graham, *Hope for the Troubled Heart* (Minneapolis: Grayson, 1991), 148.

2. Ibid., 154.

3. O. Hallesby, *Prayer* (Minneapolis: Augsburg, 1931), 77.

4. E.W. Kenyon, *In His Presence* (U.S.A.: Kenyon's Publishing Society, n.d.), 7.

5. E.M. Bounds, *The Possibilities of Prayer* (New York:

Fleming H. Revell, 1923), 43.

6. Hope MacDonald, *Discovering How to Pray* (Grand Rapids: Zondervan, 1976), 90. Used by permission of Zondervan Publishing House.

7. Charles G. Finney, *Lectures on Revivals of Religion* (Virginia Beach, Va.: CBN University Press, 1978), 58.

8. Dietrich Bonhoeffer, *The Cost of Discipleship* (New York: Macmillan, Inc., 1963), 181.

9. R.C. Sproul, *Essential Truths of the Christian Faith* (Wheaton, Ill.: Tyndale House Publishers, 1992), 252. Used by permission of Tyndale House Publishers, Inc. All rights reserved.

10. Catherine Marshall, *Adventures in Prayer* (Old Tappan, N.J.: Fleming H. Revell Co., 1975), 11.

11. H. Clay Trumbell, *Prayer: Its Nature and Scope* (Philadelphia: John D. Wattle & Co., 1896), 53.

Chapter 7 PRAYERLESSNESS AND BUSYNESS

1. E.M. Bounds, *Purpose in Prayer* (Chicago: Moody, 1979), 59.

2. From an address given to a Washington Briefing Conference sponsored by the National Association of Evangelicals.

3. Wesley Deuwel, *Mighty Prevailing Prayer* (Grand Rapids: Zondervan, 1990), 24.

4. Andrew Murray, *The Prayer Life* (Chicago: Moody n.d.), 19.

5. C.S. Lewis, *Letters to Malcolm: Chiefly on Prayer* (New York: Hardcourt, Brace & Company, 1963), 113.

6. Hope MacDonald, *Discovering How to Pray* (Grand Rapids: Zondervan, 1976), 30.

7. Ibid., 28.

8. Richard Foster, *Celebration of Discipline* (New York: Harper & Row, 1978), 18.

9. O. Hallesby, *Prayer* (Minneapolis: Augsburg, 1931), 48.

10. Charles R. Swindoll, *Growing Strong in the Seasons of Life* (Portland: Multnomah Press, 1983), 377.

11. E.M. Bounds, *Purpose in Prayer*, 59.

12. Jean Vanier, *Be Not Afraid* (New York: Paulist Press, 1975), 135.

13. Richard F. Lovelace, *Dynamics of Spiritual Life* (Downers Grove, Ill.: InterVarsity Press, 1980), 153.

14. Charles E. Hummel, *The Tyranny of the Urgent* (Chicago: InterVarsity Press, 1967), 16.

15. H. Clay Trumbell, *Prayer: Its Nature and Scope* (Philadelphia: John D. Wattle & Co., 1896), 157.

16. Eugenia Price, *A Women's Choice* (Grand Rapids: Zondervan, 1962).

Chapter 8 PRAYER AND STUDY

1. E.M. Bounds, *Power through Prayer* (Chicago: Moody, 1979), 87.

2. Elizabeth O'Connor, *Search for Silence* (Waco, Texas: Word Books, 1971), 95.

3. Dallas Willard, *The Spirit of the Disciplines* (San Francisco: Harper & Row, 1988), 184.

4. E.M. Bounds, *Power through Prayer*, 87–88.

Chapter 9 PRAYER AND PURITY

1. P.T. Forsyth, *The Soul of Prayer*, 63.

2. Oswald Chambers, *My Utmost for His Highest* (New

York: Dodd, Mead, & Co., 1961), 328.

3. Charles Colson, *The Body* (Dallas: Word, 1992), 142.

4. Frederick Buechner, *Wishful Thinking: A Theological ABC* (New York: Harper & Row, 1973), 15.

5. St. Benedict, *The Rule of St. Benedict*, ed. and trans. by Cardinal Gasquet (New York: Cooper Square Publishers, 1966), 51.

6. J. Oswald Sanders, *Prayer Power Unlimited* (Chicago: Moody Press, 1977), 90.

7. Joni Eareckson Tada, "Come before God in Purity," *Women's Devotional Bible NIV* (Grand Rapids: Zondervan Publishing House, 1990), 127.

8. John Dawson, *Healing America's Wounds* (Ventura, Calif.: Regal Books/Gospel Light, 1994), 94.

9. Ibid., 98.

Chapter 10 PRAYER AND UNITY

1. Sam Shoemaker, *Extraordinary Living for Ordinary Men* (Grand Rapids: Zondervan, 1965), 115.

2. Wesley L. Duewel, *Touch the World through Prayer* (Grand Rapids: Zondervan, 1986), 252. Used by permission of Zondervan Publishing House.

3. Andrew Murray, *With Christ in the School of Prayer* (Old Tappan, N.J.: Fleming H. Revell, 1953), 82–83.

Chapter 11 PRAYER AND SPIRIT

1. Andrew Murray, *The Prayer Life* (Chicago: Moody Press, n.d.), 21. Used by permission.

2. O. Hallesby, *Prayer* (Minneapolis: Augsburg, 1931), 176.

3. R.A. Torrey, *How to Pray* (Chicago: Moody Press, 1900), 55. Used by permission.
4. Wesley Duewel, *Touch the World through Prayer* (Grand Rapids: Zondervan, 1986), 45.
5. Catherine Marshall, *The Helper* (Waco, Texas: Chosen Books Publishing Co., 1978), 141.
6. Madame Guyon, *Experiencing the Depths of Jesus Christ* (Goleta, Calif.: Christian Books, 1975), 47.
7. Sue Richards, *Women's Devotional Bible* NIV (Grand Rapids: Zondervan, 1990), 1238.

Chapter 12 PRAYER AND COMBAT

1. John Piper, *The Pleasures of God* (Portland, Ore.: Multnomah Press, 1991), 228.
2. Billy Graham, *Hope for the Troubled Heart* (Minneapolis: Grayson, 1991), 148.
3. Jack Hayford, *Prayer Is Invading the Impossible* (Plainfield, N.J.: Logos, 1977), 18.
4. Paul Billheimer, *Destined for the Throne* (Fort Washington, Pa.: Christian Literature Crusade, 1983), 15.
5. S.D. Gordon, *Quiet Talks on Prayer* (Grand Rapids: Baker Book House, 1980), 21.
6. E.M. Bounds, *Purpose in Prayer* (Chicago: Moody, 1979), 89.
7. Andrew Murray, *The Prayer Life* (Chicago: Moody, n.d.), 27.
8. Piper, *The Pleasures of God*, 232.
9. Murray, *The Prayer Life*, 28.
10. Ibid., 27.
11. Evelyn Christenson, *Battling the Prince of Darkness* (Wheaton, Ill.: Victor Books, 1990), 131.

12. Gordon, *Quiet Talks on Prayer*, 28.
13. David Bryant, unpublished paper on *Spiritual Warfare*, Concerts of Prayer International.
14. E. Stanley Jones, *Abundant Living* (Nashville: BGEA, n.d.), 46.
15. Corrie ten Boom, *Each New Day* (Old Tappan, N.J.: Fleming H. Revell, 1977), October 17 entry.
16. O. Hallesby, *Prayer* (Minneapolis: Augsburg, 1931), 98.
17. Bounds, *Purpose in Prayer*, 10.
18. Richard Lovelace, *Dynamics of Spiritual Life* (Downers Grove, Ill.: InterVarsity Press, 1980), 155–56.
19. William Barclay, *A Spiritual Autobiography* (Grand Rapids: Wm. B. Eerdmans Publishing Co., 1975), 47.
20. Jacques Ellul, *Prayer and Modern Man*, trans. C. Edward Hopkin (New York: The Seabury Press, 1970), 162.
21. Bill Hybels, *Too Busy Not to Pray* (Downers Grove, Ill.: InterVarsity Press, 1988), 35.

Chapter 13 PRAYER AND REVIVAL
1. Armin Gesswein, from a message given at First Covenant Church, Oakland, California in 1989.
2. A.T. Pierson, *The Acts of the Apostles* (New York: The Baker & Taylor Co., 1894), 352.
3. Gesswein, from a message given at First Covenant Church, Oakland, California in 1989.
4. Cited by a brochure published by the National Prayer Committee, 1992.
5. Ibid.
6. Wesley Duewel, *Mighty Prevailing Prayer* (Grand

Rapids: Zondervan, 1990), 133.

7. David R. Mains, "Is Revival Near?" *Moody Monthly*, January 1992, 20.

8. Charles G. Finney, *Lectures on Revivals of Religion* (Virginia Beach, Va.: CBN University Press, 1978), 22–23.

9. Gesswein, "Fire in the Church," *Decision Magazine*, March 1964, 4.

10. David Bryant, *The Hope at Hand* (draft manuscript), 4.

11. John Dawson, *Healing America's Wounds* (Ventura, Calif.: Regal Books/Gospel Lights Publications, 1994), 13.

Chapter 14 PRAYER AND MISSION

1. David Bryant, *With Concerts of Prayer* (Ventura, Calif.: Regal, 1984), 73.

2. E.M. Bounds, *Purpose in Prayer* (Chicago: Moody, 1979), 66.

3. Robert Speer, "The Secret of Endless Intercession," *World Christian*, July/August 1986.

4. Andrew Murray, *State of the Church* (Fort Washington, Pa.: Christian Literature Crusade, 1983), 113.

5. David Bryant, *In the Gap* (Ventura, Calif.: Regal, 1979), 155.

6. Richard Lovelace, *Dynamics of Spiritual Life* (Downers Grove, Ill.: InterVarsity Press, 1980), 157.

7. Donald Bloesch, *The Struggle of Prayer* (San Francisco: Harper & Row, 1980), 159.

Chapter 15 PRAYER AND PROMISE

1. Armin Gesswein, from a message given at First Covenant Church, Oakland, California, 1989.

2. Ibid.
3. Dietrich Bonhoeffer, *Life Together* (New York: Harper & Row, 1954), 47.
4. E.M. Bounds, *The Possibilities of Prayer* (New York: Fleming H. Revell, 1923), 16.
5. Ibid., 126.
6. John Piper, *The Pleasures of God* (Portland, Ore.: Multnomah Press, 1991), 226–27.

Chapter 16 PRAYER AND LISTENING
1. Rosalind Rinker, *Prayer: Conversing with God* (Grand Rapids: Zondervan, 1959), 17–18.
2. Dick Eastman, *The Hour That Changes the World* (Grand Rapids: Baker Book House, 1978), 128.
3. Bill Hybels, *Too Busy Not to Pray* (Downers Grove, Ill.: InterVarsity Press, 1988), 109–10.
4. C.S. Lewis, *Letters to Malcolm: Chiefly on Prayer* (New York: Harcourt, Brace & Company, 1963), 116–17.
5. Lloyd John Ogilvie, *Praying with Power* (Ventura, Calif.: Regal Books, 1983), 21.
6. Oswald Chambers, *My Utmost for His Highest* (New York: Dodd, Mead & Co., 1961), 44.
7. David A. Hubbard, *The Problem with Prayer Is* (Wheaton, Ill.: Tyndale, 1972), 51.
8. John Dawson, *Taking Our Cities for God* (Lake Maey, Fla.: Creation House, 1989), 171.
9. Bill Hybels, *Honest to God?* (Grand Rapids: Zondervan, 1990), 26. Used by permission of Zondervan Publishing House.
10. Bill Bright, "The Great Adventure," *Worldwide Challenge*, Vol. 2, No. 3 May/June 1994, 46.

11. Donald Bloesch, *The Struggle of Prayer* (San Francisco: Harper & Row, 1980), 54.
12. Karl Barth, *Church Dogmatics*, ed. by G.W. Bromiley and T.F. Torrence, Vol. III, 3 (Edinburgh: Clark, 1957), 270.
13. Gail MacDonald, *High Call, High Privilege* (Wheaton, Ill.: Tyndale House Publishers, Inc., 1981), 33.
14. David Bryant, *The Hope at Hand* (draft manuscript), 97–98.

Chapter 17 PRAYER AND QUIETNESS
1. Evelyn Christenson, *What Happens When Women Pray* (Wheaton, Ill.: Victor, 1975), 112
2. Basilea Schlink, *More Precious Than Gold* (Carol Stream, Ill.: Creation House, 1978), 213.
3. Catherine Marshall, *Adventures in Prayer* (Tarrytown, N.Y.: Fleming H. Revell, 1985), 110–11.
4. Richard Foster, *Prayer: Finding the Heart's True Home* (San Francisco: Harper & Row, 1992), 93.
5. Amy Carmichael, *Thou Givest . . . They Gather* (London: Lutterworth Press, 1959), 43.

Chapter 18 PRAYER AND PREACHING
1. John Piper, *The Pleasures of God* (Portland, Ore.: Multnomah Press, 1991), 231.
2. E.M. Bounds, *Power through Prayer* (Chicago: Moody Press, 1979), 37.
3. Charles G. Finney, *Lectures on Revivals of Religion* (Virginia Beach, Va.: CBN University Press, 1978), 45.
4. Bounds, *Power through Prayer*, 27.

Chapter 19 PRAYER AND RELATIONSHIPS

1. Dietrich Bonhoeffer, *Life Together* (New York: Harper & Row, 1954), 86.
2. C.S. Lewis, *Letters to Malcolm: Chiefly on Prayer* (New York: Harcourt, Brace & Company, 1963), 106.

Chapter 20 PRAYER AND PRAISE

1. Charles H. Spurgeon, *Twelve Sermons on Prayer* (New York: Fleming Revell, 1890), 552.
2. Jack Hayford, *Prayer Is Invading the Impossible* (Plainfield, N.J.: Logos, 1977), 79.
3. D.L. Moody, *Prevailing Prayer* (Chicago: Moody Press, n.d.), 55–56.
4. Harold Lindsell, *When You Pray* (Grand Rapids: Baker Book House, 1969), 30.
5. Dick Eastman, *The Hour That Changes the World* (Grand Rapids: Baker Book House, 1978), 24.
6. Melva Wickman, shared with compiler in personal conversation.
7. Ralph Herring, *The Cycle of Prayer* (Wheaton, Ill.: Tyndale House Publishers, 1974), 16.
8. Henri J.M. Nouwen, *With Open Hands* (Notre Dame, Ind.: Ave Maria Press, 1972), 78. Used with permission of publishers.
9. Paul Billheimer, *Destined for the Throne* (Fort Washington, Pa.: Christian Literature Crusade, 1975), 18.
10. William Barclay, *Prayers for Young People* (New York: Harper & Row, 1963), 13.
11. Basilea Schlink, *More Precious Than Gold* (Carol Stream, Ill.: Creation House, 1978), 169.

12. Oswald Chambers, *If Ye Shall Ask* (Toronto: McClelland & Stewart Limited, 1938), 102.

Chapter 21 PRAYER AND PAIN

1. Bernard of Clairvaux, *The Love of God*, ed., James M. Houston (Portland, Ore.: Multnomah Press, 1983), 107.
2. Richard Foster, *Prayer: Finding the Heart's True Home* (San Francisco: Harper & Row, 1992), 19.
3. Corrie ten Boom, *Each New Day* (Old Tappan, N.J.: Fleming H. Revell, 1977), June 22 entry.
4. Samuel Chadwick, *The Path of Prayer* (Fort Washington, Pa.: Christian Literature Crusade, 1963), 81.
5. Billy Graham, *Hope for the Troubled Heart* (Minneapolis: Grayson, 1991), 148.
6. Ibid., 152.
7. Wesley Duewel, *Touch the World through Prayer* (Grand Rapids: Zondervan, 1986), 88.
8. John Dawson, *Taking Our Cities for God* (Lake Maey, Fl.: Creation House, 1989), 203.
9. Basilea Schlink, *More Precious Than Gold* (Carol Stream, Ill.: Creation House, 1978), 26.
10. Oswald Chambers, *If Ye Shall Ask* (Toronto: McClelland & Stewart Limited, 1938), 103.

Chapter 22 PRAYER AND PERSEVERANCE

1. Hope MacDonald, *Discovering How to Pray* (Grand Rapids: Zondervan, 1976), 86.
2. Frederick Buechner, *Wishful Thinking: A Theological ABC* (New York: Harper & Row, 1973), 70.
3. Andrew Murray, *With Christ in the School of Prayer*

(Old Tappan, N.J.: Fleming H. Revell, 1953), 87–88.

4. Billy Graham, *Hope for the Troubled Heart* (Minneapolis: Grayson, 1991), 149.

5. Jack Hayford, *Prayer Is Invading the Impossible* (Plainfield, N.J.: Logos, 1977), 141.

6. Edith Schaeffer, "Restoring Vitality in Your Prayer Life: An Interview with Edith Schaeffer," interviewer, Bonne Steffen, *Intercessor for America Newsletter*, Vol. 20 No. 1, January 1993.

7. Bill Hybels, *Too Busy Not to Pray* (Downers Grove, Ill.: InterVarsity Press, 1988), 35.

Chapter 23 PRAYER AND SCRIPTURE

1. Armin Gesswein, from a message given at First Covenant Church, Oakland, California in 1989.

2. Ibid.

3. Andrew Murray, *The Prayer Life* (Chicago: Moody Press, n.d.), 107.

4. Dick Eastman, *The Hour That Changes the World* (Grand Rapids: Baker Book House, 1978), 57.

5. Gesswein, from a message given at First Covenant Church, Oakland, California in 1989.

6. Dietrich Bonhoeffer, *Life Together* (New York: Harper & Row, 1954), 84.

7. Andrew Murray, *With Christ in the School of Prayer* (Old Tappan, N.J.: Fleming H. Revell, 1953), 182.

Chapter 24 PRAYER AND GRACE

1. Karl Barth, *Prayer and Preaching* (London: SCM Press LTD., 1964), 16.

2. Richard Foster, *Prayer: Finding the Heart's True*

Home (San Francisco: Harper & Row, 1992), 8.

3. David Bryant, *Concerts of Prayer International* 1992 *Ministry Report*, 5.
4. Roger Palms, *Enjoying the Closeness of God* (Minneapolis: Worldwide Publications, 1989), 68.
5. A.W. Tozer, *The Pursuit of God* (Harrisburg, Pa.: Christian Publications, n.d.), 11–12.
6. J.I. Packer, "The Lamb upon His Throne," *Tabletalk* (Lake Mary, Fla.: Ligonier Publications, December 1992), 15.
7. Tozer, *The Pursuit of God*, 12.
8. Bryant, *The Hope at Hand* (draft manuscript), 56.
9. Ibid., 70–71.
10. John White, *Daring to Draw Near* (Downer's Grove, Ill.: InterVarsity Press, 1977), 8
11. John Dawson, *Healing America's Wounds* (Ventura, Calif.: Regal Books/Gospel Light Publications, 1994), 13–14.

Chapter 25 PRAYER IN SECRET
1. Armin Gesswein, from a message given at First Covenant Church, Oakland, California, 1989.
2. Leonard Ravenhill, "Prayer" (Lindale, Texas: Pretty Good Publications, 1992).
3. Andrew Murray, *With Christ in the School of Prayer* (Old Tappan, N.J.: Fleming H. Revell, 1953), 23.
4. Catherine Marshall, *Adventures in Prayer* (Old Tappan, N.J.: Fleming H. Revell, 1975), 78.

Chapter 26 PRAYER IN PRACTICE
1. Armin Gesswein, from a message given at First Covenant Church, Oakland, California, 1989.

2. S.D. Gordon, *Quiet Talks on Prayer* (Grand Rapids: Baker Book House, 1980), 12.

3. E. Stanley Jones, *Abundant Living* (Nashville: Abingdon Press, 1942), 47.

4. E.M. Bounds, *Purpose in Prayer* (Chicago: Moody Press, 1979), 28.

5. Jack Hayford, *Prayer Is Invading the Impossible* (Plainfield, N.J.: Logos, 1977), 143.

Chapter 27 PRAYER IN PARTNERSHIP

1. Andrew Murray, *State of the Church* (Fort Washington, Pa.: Christian Literature Crusade, 1983), 63.

2. A.W. Tozer, *The Pursuit of God* (Harrisburg, Pa.: Christian Publications, n.d.), 45.

3. Oswald Chambers, *My Utmost for His Highest* (New York: Dodd, Mead & Co., 1961), 222.

4. Wesley Duewel, *Touch the World through Prayer* (Grand Rapids: Zondervan, 1986), 41.

5. Jack Hayford, *Prayer Is Invading the Impossible* (Plainfield, N.J.: Logos, 1977), 125.

6. Madeleine L'Engle, "The Gift of Prayer," A.D., April 1980, 28.

7. Evelyn Underhill, *The Evelyn Underhill Reader*, compiled by Thomas S. Kepler (Nashville: Abingdon Press, 1962), 165.

8. Catherine Marshall, *The Helper* (Waco, Texas: Chosen Books, 1978), 140.

9. Rosalind Rinker, *Women's Devotional Bible* NIV (Grand Rapids: Zondervan Publishing House, 1990), 1050.

10. Ibid., 1090.

11. P.T. Forsyth, *The Soul of Prayer*, 32.

12. Donald Bloesch, *The Struggle of Prayer* (San Francisco: Harper & Row, 1980), 55–56.

Chapter 28 PRAYER UNANSWERED
1. P.T. Forsyth, *The Soul of Prayer*, 14.
2. C.S. Lewis, *Letters to Malcolm: Chiefly on Prayer* (New York: Harcourt, Brace & Company, 1963), 28.
3. Ibid., 58.
4. Richard Foster, *Prayer: Finding the Heart's True Home* (San Francisco: Harper & Row, 1992), 182.
5. Oswald Chambers, *My Utmost for His Highest* (New York: Dodd, Mead & Co., 1961), 219.
6. Billy Graham, *Hope for the Troubled Heart* (Minneapolis: Grayson, 1991), 158.
7. Ibid., 143.
8. Oswald Chambers, *If Ye Shall Ask* (Toronto: McClelland & Stewart, Limited, 1938), 47.
9. Mrs. Charles E. Cowman, "Training in the Faith Life," *Women's Devotional Bible* NIV (Grand Rapids: Zondervan, 1990), 1082.

Chapter 29 PRAYER FROM GOD'S PERSPECTIVE
1. Robert Boyd Munger, *My Heart Christ's Home* (Downer's Grove, Ill.: InterVarsity Press, 1986), 16.
2. E.W. Kenyon, *In His Presence* (U.S.A.: Kenyon's Gospel Publishing Society, n.d.), 6.
3. Munger, *My Heart Christ's Home*, 16.
4. Bill Bright, "The Great Adventure," *Worldwide Challenge*, Vol. 2 No. 3, May/June 1994, 46.
5. Stephen Verney, quoted by Joyce Huggett in *The*

Joy of Listening to God (Downers Grove, Ill.: InterVarsity Press, 1986), 70.

Chapter 30 PRAYER AND FASTING
1. Richard Foster, *Celebration of Discipline* (New York: Harper & Row, 1992), 52.
2. Derek Prince, *Restoration through Fasting* (Fort Lauderdale, Fla.: Derek Prince Publications, 1970), 12.
3. Dallas Willard, *The Spirit of the Disciplines* (San Francisco: Harper & Row, 1988), 166.
4. Arthur Wallis, *God's Chosen Fast* (Fort Washington, Pa.: Christian Literature Crusade, 1986), 40.
5. Wesley Duewel, *Mighty Prevailing Prayer* (Grand Rapids: Zondervan, 1990), 181.
6. Dr. Joon Gon Kim, quoted in a message given at the International Prayer Assembly in Seoul, Korea, June 1984.

Chapter 31 PRAYER AND HUMILITY
1. Henri J.M. Nouwen, *Clowning in Rome* (Garden City, N.Y.: Image, 1979), 73.
2. Thomas Kelly, *A Testament of Devotion* (San Francisco: Harper, 1992), 54.
3. Richard Foster, *Prayer: Finding the Heart's True Home* (San Francisco: Harper & Row, 1992), 9.
4. John Piper, *The Pleasures of God* (Portland, Ore.: Multnomah Press, 1991), 221.
5. Catherine Marshall, *Adventures in Prayer* (Old Tappan, N.J.: Revell, 1975), 1.
6. Elizabeth Larsen, shared with compiler in personal conversation.

7. Thomas Merton, quoted by Joyce Huggett in *The Joy of Listening to God* (Downers Grove, Ill.: InterVarsity Press, 1986), 57.

Chapter 32 PRAYER AND HEALING
1. E.M. Bounds, *The Possibilities of Prayer* (New York: Fleming H. Revell, 1923), 46.
2. Richard Foster, *Prayer: Finding the Heart's True Home* (San Francisco: Harper & Row, 1992), 204.
3. Dr. Alexis Carrel, *Prayer* (New York: Morehouse-Gorham Co., 1948), 37–38.
4. Arthur Wallis, *God's Chosen Fast* (Fort Washington, Pa.: Christian Literature Crusade, 1986), 80.

Chapter 33 PRAYER AND ALERTNESS
1. C.S. Lewis, *Letters to Malcolm: Chiefly on Prayer* (New York: Harcourt, Brace & Company, 1963), 16.
2. George Mallone, *Arming for Spiritual Warfare* (Downers Grove, Ill.: InterVarsity Press, 1991), 34.
3. Charles Finney, *Lectures on Revivals of Religion* (Virginia Beach, Va.: CBN University Press, 1978), 97.
4. Curtis Mitchell, *Praying Jesus' Way* (Old Tappan, N.J.: Revell, 1977), 79–80.

Chapter 34 PRAYER AND HOPE
1. Henri J.M. Nouwen, *With Open Hands* (Notre Dame, Ind.: Ave Maria Press, 1972), 84.
2. Rebecca Manley Pippert, *Hope Has Its Reasons* (San Francisco: Harper & Row, 1989), 194.
3. Frederick Buechner, *Wishful Thinking: A Theological

ABC (New York: Harper & Row, 1973), 71.

4. Jack Hayford, *Prayer Is Invading the Impossible* (Plainfield, N.J.: Logos, 1977), 107.

5. David Bryant, *With Concerts of Prayer* (Ventura, Calif.: Regal, 1984), 212.

6. David Bryant, *The Hope at Hand* (draft manuscript), 10.

7. Donald Bloesch, *The Struggle of Prayer* (San Francisco: Harper & Row, 1980), 169–70.

BIBLIOGRAPHY

✦ ✦ ✦

Aquinas, Thomas. *On Prayer and the Contemplative Life*.
London: R & T Washbourne, Ltd., 1914.

Barclay, William. *Prayers for Young People*. New York:
Harper & Row, 1963.
_____. *A Spiritual Biography*. Grand Rapids: Wm. B.
Eerdmans Publishing Co., 1975.
Barth, Karl. *Church Dogmatics*. Ed., G.W. Bromiley and
T.F. Torrence. Vol. III, 3. Edinburgh: Clark, 1957.
_____. *Prayer*. Trans., Sara F. Terrien. Philadelphia:
Westminster Press, 1952.
_____. *Prayer and Preaching*. London: SCM Press
Ltd., 1964.
Benedict, *The Rule of St. Benedict*. Ed. and trans., Cardi-
nal Gasquet. New York: Cooper Square Publishers,
1966.
Bernard of Clairvaux. *The Love of God*. Ed. James M.
Houston. Portland, Ore.: Multnomah Press, 1983.
Billheimer, Paul. *Destined for the Throne*. Fort Washing-

ton, Pa.: Christian Literature Crusade, 1975.

Bloesch, Donald G. *The Struggle of Prayer*. San Francisco: Harper & Row, 1980.

Bonhoeffer, Dietrich. *The Cost of Discipleship*. New York: Macmillan, Inc., 1963.

_____. *Life Together*. New York: Harper & Row, 1954.

Booth-Tucker, F. de L. *Memoirs of Catherine Booth*. Vol. 2. New York: Fleming H. Revell Company, 1892.

Bounds, E.M. *The Possibilities of Prayer*. New York: Fleming H. Revell, 1923.

_____. *Power through Prayer*. Chicago: Moody Press, 1979.

_____. *Purpose in Prayer*. Chicago: Moody Press, 1980.

Bright, Bill. "The Great Adventure," *Worldwide Challenge* 21 No. 3 (May/June 1994).

Bryant, David. *The Hope at Hand*. Grand Rapids: Baker Book House, 1995.

_____. *In the Gap*. Ventura, Calif.: Regal, 1979.

_____. *With Concerts of Prayer*. Ventura, Calif.: Regal, 1984.

Buechner, Frederick. *Wishful Thinking: A Theological ABC*. New York: Harper & Row, 1973.

Carmichael, Amy. *Thou Givest . . . They Gather*. London: Lutterworth Press, 1959.

Carrel, Alexis. *Prayer*. New York: Morehouse-Gorham Co., 1948.

Castle, Tony, ed. *The New Book of Christian Quotations*. New York: Crossroad Publishing, 1988.

Chadwick, Samuel. *The Path of Prayer*. Kansas City: Beacon Hill, 1931.

Chambers, Oswald. *If Ye Shall Ask*. Toronto: McClelland & Stewart Limited, 1938.

_____. *My Utmost for His Highest*. New York: Dodd, Mead & Co., 1961.

Christenson, Evelyn. *Battling the Prince of Darkness*. Wheaton, Ill.: Victor Books, 1990.

_____. *What Happens When Women Pray*. Wheaton, Ill.: Victor Books, 1975.

Colson, Charles. *The Body*. Dallas: Word, 1992.

Dawson, John. *Healing America's Wounds*. Ventura, Calif.: Gospel Light/Regal Books, 1994.

_____. *Taking Our Cities for God*. Lake Maey, Fla.: Creation House, 1989.

Day, Albert Edward. *Discipline and Discovery*. Springdale, Pa.: Whitaker House, 1988.

Doan, Eleanor L., compiler. *431 Quotes from the Notes of Henrietta C. Mears*. Glendale, Calif.: Regal Books/Gospel Light Publications, 1970.

Draper, Edythe, compiler. *Draper's Book of Quotations for the Christian World*. Wheaton, Ill.: Tyndale House Publishers, 1992.

Duewel, Wesley L. *Mighty Prevailing Prayer*. Grand Rapids: Zondervan, 1990.

_____. *Touch the World through Prayer*. Grand Rapids: Zondervan, 1986.

Dunnam, Maxie. *The Workbook of Intercessory Prayer*. Nashville: The Upper Room, 1979.

Eastman, Dick. *The Hour That Changes the World*. Grand Rapids: Baker Book House, 1978.

Eckhart, Meister. *Meister Eckhart*. Ed. and trans. Raymond Blakney. New York: Harper, 1941.

Ellul, Jacques. *Prayer and Modern Man*. Trans. C. Edward Hopkin. New York: The Seabury Press, 1970.

Finney, Charles G. *Lectures on Revivals of Religion*. Virginia Beach, Va.: CBN University Press, 1978.

_____. *Recapturing Biblical Intercession*. Memphis: Prayer-Resources, 1982.

Forsyth, P.T. *The Soul of Prayer*. Grand Rapids: Eerdmans, 1916.

Foster, Richard. *Celebration of Discipline*. New York: Harper & Row, 1978.

_____. *Freedom of Simplicity*. New York: Harper & Row, 1981.

_____. *Prayer: Finding the Heart's True Home*. San Francisco: Harper & Row, 1992.

Gesswein, Armin. "Fire in the Church," *Decision Magazine* (March 1964).

_____. *With One Accord in One Place*. Harrisburg, Pa.: Christian Publications, Inc., 1978.

Gordon, S.D. *Quiet Talks on Prayer*. Grand Rapids: Baker Book House, 1980.

Graham, Billy. *Hope for the Troubled Heart*. Minneapolis: Grayson, 1991.

_____. "Prayer" (tract). Minneapolis: Billy Graham Evangelistic Association, n.d.

Guyon, Madame. *Experiencing the Depths of Jesus Christ*. Goleta, Calif.: Christian Books, 1975.

Hallesby, O. *Prayer*. Minneapolis: Augsburg Publishing House, 1931.

Halverson, Richard C. *Intercessors for America Newsletter* 13 No. 4 (April 1986).

Hammerskjold, Dag. *Markings*, Trans. Leif Sjoberg and W.H. Auden. New York: Alfred A. Knopf, Inc., 1964.

Hasler, Richard A., compiler. *Journal of Prayer: An Anthology*. Valley Forge, Pa.: Judson Press, 1982.

Hayford, Jack. *Prayer Is Invading the Impossible*. Plainfield, N.J.: Logos, 1977.

Herring, Ralph. *The Cycle of Prayer*. Wheaton, Ill.: Tyndale House Publishers, 1974.

Holmes, Marjorie. *How Can I Find God?* Garden City, N.Y.: Doubleday & Company Inc., 1975.

Hubbard, David A. *The Problem with Prayer Is*. Wheaton, Ill.: Tyndale, 1972.

Hummel, Charles E. *The Tyranny of the Urgent*. Downers Grove, Ill.: InterVarsity Press, 1967.

Hybels, Bill. *Honest to God*. Grand Rapids: Zondervan, 1990.

_____. *Too Busy Not to Pray*. Downers Grove, Ill.: InterVarsity Press, 1988.

Jones, E. Stanley. *Abundant Living*. Nashville: Abingdon Press, 1942.

Kelly, Thomas. *A Testament of Devotion*. New York: Harper & Row, 1941.

Kenyon, E.W. *In His Presence*. U.S.A. Kenyon's Gospel Publishing Society, n.d.

Kepler, Thomas S., compiler. *The Evelyn Underhill Reader*. Nashville: Abingdon Press, 1962.

The Kneeling Christian. Edinburgh, London: Marshall, Morgan & Scott, Limited, n.d.

Lavender, John Allan. *Why Prayers Are Unanswered*. Valley Forge, Pa.: Judson Press, 1967.

Law, William. *A Serious Call to a Devout and Holy Life*. Philadelphia: Westminster Press, 1955.

Lawrence, Brother. *Practice of the Presence of God*. Old Tappan, N.J.: Revell, 1956.

Lechman, Judith C. *The Spirituality of Gentleness: Growing toward Christian Wholeness*. New York: Harper & Row, 1987.

Leech, Bryan Jeffery. "The Lord's Prayer" (unpublished article), (December 1992).

L'Engle, Madeline. "The Gift of Prayer," A.D. (April 1980).

Lewis, C.S. *Letters to Malcolm: Chiefly on Prayer*. New York: Harcourt, Brace & Company, 1963.

Lindsell, Harold. *When You Pray*. Grand Rapids: Baker Book House, 1969.

Lovelace, Richard F. *Dynamics of Spiritual Life*. Downers Grove, Ill.: InterVarsity Press, 1980.

MacArthur, John, Jr. *Jesus' Pattern of Prayer*. Chicago: Moody Press, 1981.

MacDonald, Gail. *High Call, High Privilege*. Wheaton, Ill.: Tyndale House Publishers, 1981.

MacDonald, Gordon. *Ordering Your Private World*. Nashville: Thomas Nelson, 1984.

MacDonald, Hope. *Discovering How to Pray*. Grand Rapids: Zondervan, 1976.

Mains, David R. "Is Revival Near?" *Moody Monthly* (January 1992).

Mains, Karen Burton. *With My Whole Heart*. Portland, Ore.: Multnomah Press, 1987.

Mallone, George. *Arming for Spiritual Warfare*. Downers Grove, Ill.: InterVarsity Press, 1991.

Marshall, Catherine. *Adventures in Prayer*. Old Tappan, N.J.: Revell, 1975.

_____. *The Helper*. Waco, Texas: Chosen Books Publishing Co., Ltd., 1978.

Mitchell, Curtis C. *Praying Jesus' Way*. Old Tappan, N.J.: Revell, 1977.

Moody, D.L. *Prevailing Prayer*. Chicago: Moody, n.d.

Muggeridge, Malcolm. *Something Beautiful for God*. Garden City, N.Y.: Image, 1977.

Munger, Robert Boyd. *My Heart Christ's Home*. Downer's Grove, Ill.: InterVarsity Press, 1986.

Murray, Andrew. *The Prayer Life*. Chicago: Moody, n.d.

_____. *State of the Church*. Fort Washington, Pa.: Christian Literature Crusade, 1983.

_____. *With Christ in the School of Prayer*. Old Tappan, N.J.: Fleming H. Revell, 1953.

Nee, Watchman. *The Prayer Ministry of the Church*. New York: Christian Fellowship Publications, 1973.

Nouwen, Henri, J.M. *Clowning in Rome*. Garden City, N.Y.: Image, 1979.

_____. *With Open Hands*. Notre Dame, Ind.: Ave Maria Press, 1972.

O'Connor, Elizabeth. *Search for Silence*. Waco, Texas: Word Books, 1971.

Ogilvie, John Lloyd. *Praying with Power*. Ventura, Calif.: Regal Books, 1983.

Packer, J.I. "The Lamb Upon His Throne," *Tabletalk* 16 No. 12 (December 1992).

Palms, Roger C. *Enjoying the Closeness of God*. Minneapolis: Worldwide Publications, 1989.

Parker, Dr. William R. and Elaine St. Johns. *Prayer Can Change Your Life*. Englewood Cliffs, N.J.: Prentice-Hall, Inc., 1957.

Peale, Norman Vincent, et al. *What Prayer Can Do*. Garden City, N.Y.: Doubleday & Co. 1953.

Peterson, Eugene H. *Answering God*. San Francisco: Harper & Row, 1989.

Pierson, A.T. *The New Acts of the Apostles*. New York: The Baker & Taylor Co., 1894.

Piper, John. *The Pleasures of God*. Portland, Ore.: Multnomah Press, 1991.

Pippert, Rebecca. *Hope Has Its Reasons*. San Francisco: Harper & Row, 1989.

Prince, Derek. *Restoration through Fasting*. Derek Prince Publications, 1970.

Ravenhill, Leonard. *Prayer*. Lindale, Texas: Pretty Good Publishing, 1992.

Rinker, Rosalind. *Prayer: Conversing with God*. Grand Rapids: Zondervan, 1959.

Sanders, J. Oswald. *Prayer Power Unlimited*. Chicago: Moody, 1977.

Schaeffer, Edith. "Restoring Vitality in Your Prayer Life: An Interview with Edith Schaeffer." Interviewed by Bonne Steffen. *Intercessors for America Newsletter* 20 No. 1 (Jan. 1993).

Schaff, Philip, ed. *The Creeds of Christendom*. Vol. 3. New York: Harper, 1919.

Schlink, Basilea. *More Precious Than Gold*. Carol

Stream, Ill.: Creation House, 1978.

Shoemaker, Sam. *Extraordinary Living for Ordinary Men*. Grand Rapids: Zondervan, 1965.

Speer, Robert E. "The Secret of Endless Intercession," *World Christian* (July/August 1986).

Sproul, R.C. *Essential Truths of the Christian Faith*. Wheaton, Ill.: Tyndale House Publishers, 1992.

Spurgeon, C.H. *Lectures to My Students*. Grand Rapids: Baker Book House, 1977.

_____. *Twelve Sermons on Prayer*. New York: Fleming H. Revell, 1890.

Sweeting, George, ed. *Great Quotes and Illustrations*. Waco, Texas: Word Publishing, 1985.

Swindoll, Charles R. *Growing Strong in the Seasons of Life*. Portland, Ore.: Multnomah Press, 1983.

ten Boom, Corrie. *Each New Day*. Old Tappan, N.J.: Fleming H. Revell, 1977.

Teresa, Mother. *A Gift for God*. New York: Harper & Row Publishers, 1975.

Tirabassi, Becky. *Releasing God's Power*. Nashville: Thomas Nelson, 1990.

Torrey, R.A. *How to Pray*. Chicago: Moody, 1900.

Tozer, A.W. *The Pursuit of God*. Harrisburg, Pa.: Christian Publications, n.d.

Trumbell, H. Clay. *Prayer: Its Nature and Scope*. Philadelphia: John D. Wattles & Co., 1896.

Vanier, Jean. *Be Not Afraid*. New York: Paulist Press, 1975.

Wallis, Arthur. *God's Chosen Fast*. Fort Washington, Pa.:

Christian Literature Crusade, 1975.

Wallis, Charles L., ed. *The Treasure Chest*. New York: Harper & Row, 1965.

White, John. *Daring to Draw Near*. Downers Grove, Ill.: InterVarsity Press, 1977.

Willard, Dallas. *The Spirit of the Disciplines*. San Francisco: Harper & Row, 1988.

Women's Devotional Bible NIV. Grand Rapids: Zondervan Publishing House, 1990.

AUTHOR INDEX

✦ ✦ ✦

M

N

O

P

R